ポーセリンアートの和モダンテクニック

作品づくりのための装飾アイディア

Evolution of Porcelain

Elucidation of Novel Decoration Techniques

花島悦子
Etsuko Hanajima

日貿出版社

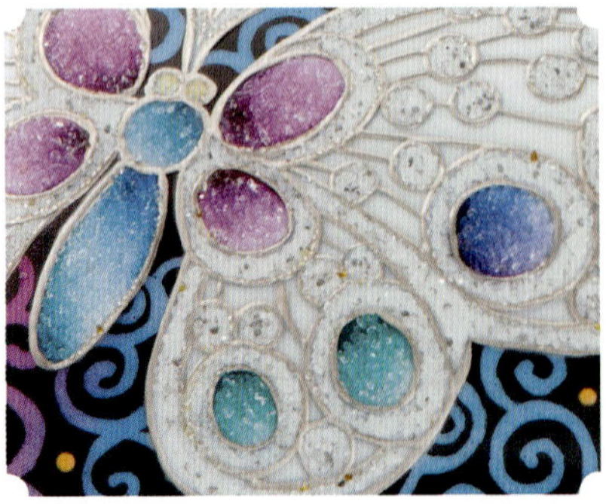

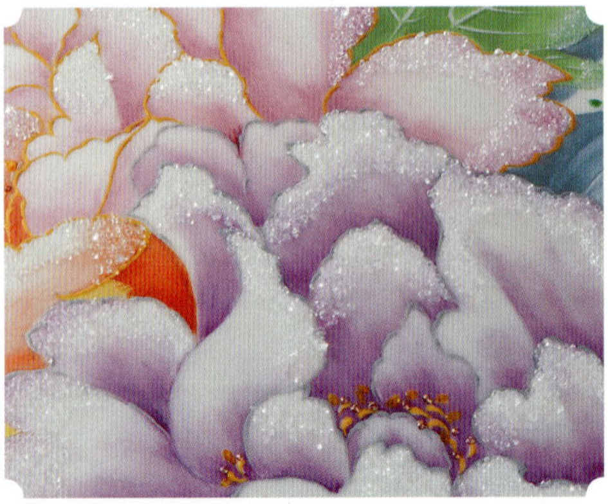

はじめに

2011年に日貿出版社から刊行した初めての著書『ポーセリン・アートの装飾テクニック』が幸いにも多くの方々からご好評をいただき、このたび、その続編ともいえる本書を上梓することとなりました。

この本では、前著でご紹介できなかったガラスビーズ装飾やイリデッセント絵の具を使った作品づくり、また前著でも紹介したイングレーズ絵の具やラスター、メタリック絵の具、エナメルフリット、スクラッチ技法などをさらに幅広く応用したアイディアとテクニックについて詳しく解説しています。

一つ一つの材料やテクニックは特別に目新しいものではないかもしれません。しかし、それらの使い方、組み合わせ方によって思いもよらぬ面白い表現ができることがあります。それが私にとってのポーセリン・ペインティングの醍醐味であり、その感動を読者の皆様にお伝えできたらと思います。

なお、本書には英文訳を併載しておりますが、大意訳であり、一部本文と異なる場合があることをご了承下さい。

2014年7月

花島 悦子

Preface

In 2011, my first book, *The Eclectic Sense of East-West Porcelain Art Decoration* (*Porcelain Art no Soshoku Techniques*) was published and I felt extremely honored that it was well received by porcelain painters all over the world. This has inspired and encouraged me to publish this new book.

In this book, the innovative usages and applications of "enamel frit," "scratch technique," "in-glaze paints" and "luster" are described. The combination of usual techniques with "glass-beading," "metallic paints" and "iridescent paints" are also demonstrated.

Each technique by itself is not so new but combined together show another face from a different angle of harmony and beauty. This is the fun part of porcelain painting for me which I would like to share with the readers.

July 2014

Etsuko Hanajima

Contents

はじめに　Preface — 3

1章［作品］　Chapter 1　Collection of Works — 5

伊万里風牡丹皿　Grand Imari — 6
四季の舞扇　Four Seasons — 8
菊の丸窓　Round Windows of Chrysanthemums — 10
花園の鶴　Celestial Cranes — 12
紅椿　Red Camellia — 14
青のハーモニー　Peonies in Blue Harmony — 16
沖の鶴　A Crane on the Sea — 17
深海に牡丹　Peonies in the Deep Ocean — 18
宇宙のクリスマス　Cosmic Christmas — 19
暁の蓮　Heavenly Lotus — 20
輝きの時　Golden Moment — 21
夕暮れの藤　Evening Wisteria — 22
花の集い　Floral Harmony in a Box — 24
椿のティーセット　Camellias on Tea Set — 25
紫陽花の花束　Hydrangea Bouquet — 26
籠の蝶々　Butterflies in a Basket — 28
蝶の宝石　Jeweled Butterfly — 29
牡丹狂乱　Strange-looking Peonies — 30
朝露とクレマチス　Clematis with Dewdrops — 32
舞扇　Fans for Japanese Dance — 33
牡丹のコサージュ　Peony Corsage — 34
更紗牡丹　Chiffon Peonies — 35
睡蓮と鯉　Carp with Water Lilies — 36

2章［テクニック紹介］　Chapter 2　Techniques — 37

ガラスビーズ装飾のアイディアとテクニック
Ideas and techniques with glass-beading — 38

主な材料　The materials — 39
作品づくりの手順　The process of glass-beading — 40
焼成方法　The firing of glass-beading — 40
応用テクニック　The applications with glass-beading — 40
注意点とトラブル対処法　Cautions and trouble-shooting — 41
ガラスビーズ装飾の基本　The basic of the glass-beading — 42
いろいろな大きさのビーズを分けて付ける
Apply glass beads of different sizes on separated places — 44
いろいろな大きさのビーズを混ぜて付ける
Apply glass beads M and L on the same place — 45

ラスターを使ったアイディアとテクニック
Ideas and techniques with luster — 46

ラスターの不思議　Mystical luster — 46
ラスターとイングレーズ絵の具　Luster on in-glaze paints — 46
ラスターの重ね塗り　The double coats with lusters — 46
ラスターと金の組み合わせ
The combination with luster and gold — 47
ラスターとメタリック絵の具の組み合わせ
The combination with luster and metallic paints — 47
ラスターの墨はじき　Masking with Indian ink — 48

メタリック絵の具のアイディアとテクニック
Ideas and techniques with metallic paints — 50

メタリック絵の具と上絵の具の組み合わせ
Combination with paints — 50
無色ラスターとメタリック絵の具の組み合わせ
The combination with white luster — 51
メタリックゴールドの上に絵の具で描く
Painting on metallic gold texture — 52
メタリックゴールドによる蒔絵風のテクスチャー
The gold enamel work looks like lacquer work — 53

イリデッセントのアイディアとテクニック
Ideas and techniques with iridescent paints — 54

イングレーズの応用　Applications of in-glaze painting — 56

イングレーズの基本　The basic of the in-glaze technique — 56
呉須で描くイングレーズ　Paint on glaze with *gosu* — 58
イングレーズとラスター　In-glaze painting with luster — 59

和のモチーフを描く　Painting traditional Japanese patterns — 60

鯉と蓮の葉の皿　Carp and Lotus Leaves — 60
霜降り模様の鶴の皿　A Crane with Frosty Texture — 64
牡丹の丸皿　A Peony with Black Rope — 68
伝統の文様を描く　Drawing traditional Japanese patterns — 71

スタディー1　宇宙のクリスマス　{Study 1} Cosmic Christmas — 72
スタディー2　暁の蓮　{Study 2} Heavenly Lotus — 75
スタディー3　沖の鶴　{Study 3} A Crane on the Sea — 78

私が使う基本の道具　Basic tools and materials — 80
窯と焼成　Kiln and Firing — 86
掲載作品に使用した絵の具と特殊材料一覧
List of painting colors and materials — 88
下絵集　Sketch Collection — 91
絵付けの用具・材料取扱店　Tools and materials shop list — 109
おわりに　Gratitude — 110
著者略歴　Profile — 111

1章［作品］
Chapter 1　Collection of Works

伊万里風牡丹皿 Grand Imari D 35.5 cm

花の周りのイングレーズの部分を最初に焼成してからラスターを塗り、その後、上絵付けの部分を描きました。
花びらと葉の縁取りは金盛りではなく、ドット付きの金線です。

The in-glaze part was done first. Luster and regular painting followed.
The outline of the petals and leaves was done with dotting gold lines around them.

※91頁に下絵を掲載。
The line drawing is on p. 91.

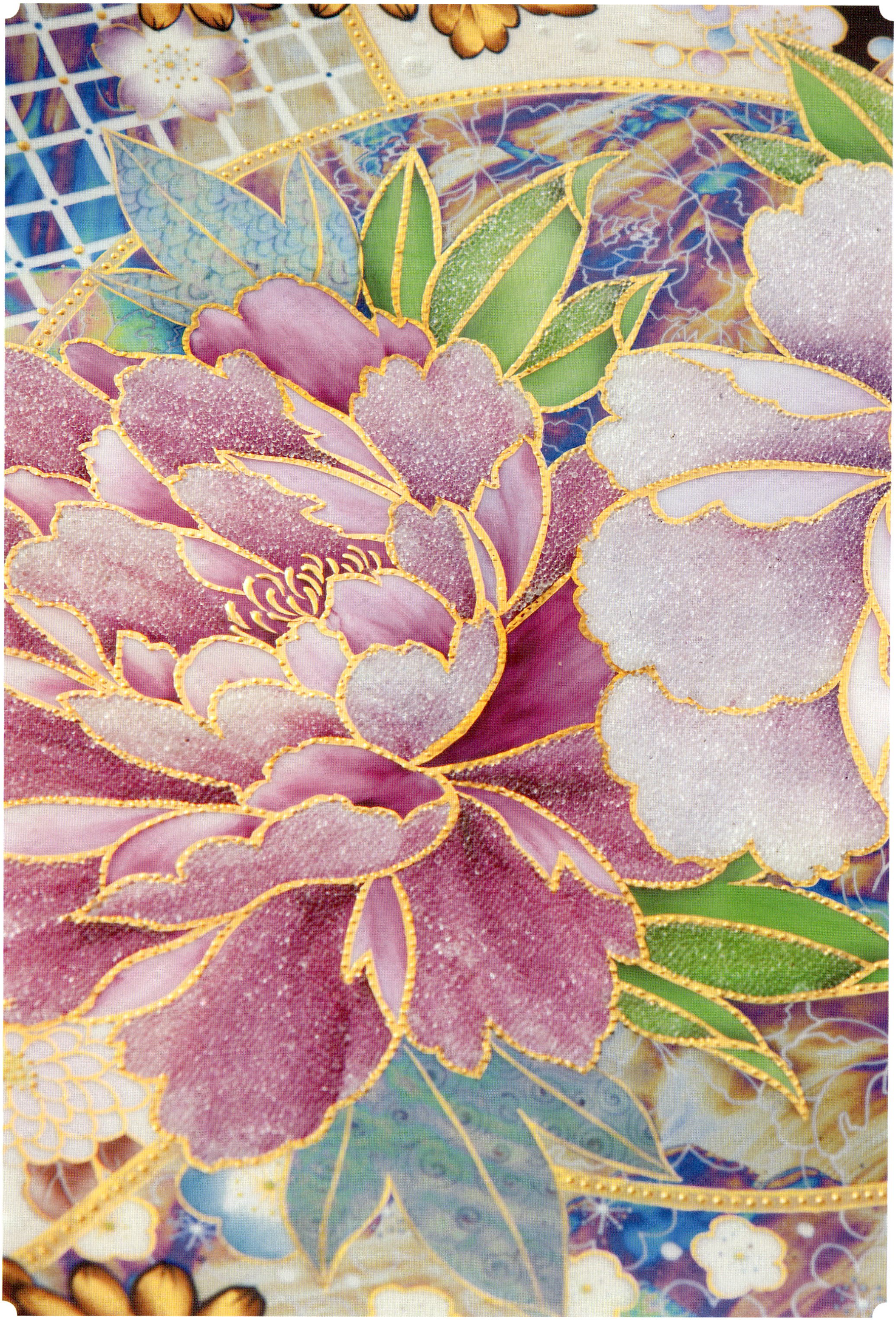

四季の舞扇　Four Seasons　34.8 × 34.8 cm

扇の骨の部分はマット金の下地に真珠ラスターを重ね塗りしました。
背景のグレーの帯は黒地にSサイズのガラスビーズを焼き付けて表現しました。

The handles of the fans were done with luster on gold.
The gray ribbon on the black background was done with small glass beads.

※92頁に下絵を掲載。
The line drawing is on p. 92.

9

菊の丸窓　Round Windows of Chrysanthemums　D 40.0 cm

背景は丸窓の部分を残してイングレーズ焼成を行い、その上にラスターを塗っています。
金色の葉は、焼成後のマット金に水色ラスターを塗り、その上にマーブルローションをかけて焼成しました。

The in-glaze part was done first, followed by luster painting.
Gold leaves were done with blue luster and marble lotion on the gold.

11

鶴の背景の花々の表現にはメタリック絵の具やメタリックエナメルを多用しています。
蒔絵風の菊の描き方については53頁、牡丹の葉については51頁、鶴については65〜67頁をご覧下さい。

花園の鶴　Celestial Cranes　D 36.5 cm

The texture was made by using metallic gold and metallic enamel.
Refer to pages 51, 53 and 65-67.

13

背景のイングレーズの部分には焼成後、真珠ラスターを乗せています。
黒いリボンの部分はオーロララスターを下地に塗り、マットブラックを塗ってスクラッチで模様を描いています。

紅椿　Red Camellia　D 35.5 cm

背景のイングレーズの部分には焼成後、真珠ラスターを乗せています。
黒いリボンの部分はオーロララスターを下地に塗り、マットブラックを塗ってスクラッチで模様を描いています。

The in-glaze part was over-painted with luster. Checkers was done with blue luster, metallic white and enamel.
The black ribbon was done with scratched mat black paint on the aurora luster.

15

青のハーモニー　Peonies in Blue Harmony　D 30.5 cm

背景のマット金は、スポンジでパディングすることにより、なめらかな質感を出しました。
The gold area of the background was done by padding the mat gold.

※93頁に下絵を掲載。
The line drawing is on p. 93.

沖の鶴　A Crane on the Sea　D 31.2 cm

皿の縁の文様はイングレーズ絵の具とラスターで、中央の部分は上絵の具で描いています。
The design of the border was painted with in-glaze paints and luster.
The design of the center was painted with regular paints.

※縁の装飾の制作方法解説は78〜79頁、下絵は94〜96頁に掲載。
Refer to p. 78-79 how to paint the border design of this piece. The line drawing is on p. 94-96.

背景は、食品用のラップを使ってイングレーズ絵の具のアガットブルーでテクスチャーを作り、
焼成後その上に水色ラスターを乗せて、深海のイメージを表現しました。
銀の葉は焼成後のマットプラチナにロイヤルバイオレットで影をつけて描きました。

深海に牡丹　Peonies in the Deep Ocean　D 40.0 cm

背景は、食品用のラップを使ってイングレーズ絵の具のアガットブルーでテクスチャーを作り、
焼成後その上に水色ラスターを乗せて、深海のイメージを表現しました。
銀の葉は焼成後のマットプラチナにロイヤルバイオレットで影をつけて描きました。

The blue luster was applied to create the texture of the background which was done with in-glaze paint and with cling film.
The silver leaves were done by painting Royal Violet on the mat platinum.

宇宙のクリスマス　Cosmic Christmas　D 27.2 cm

下地に真珠ラスターを塗って焼成してから、墨汁を使った墨はじき（48頁参照）のテクニックで背景の模様を描き、水色ラスターを乗せました。水溶性のスクラッチリキッドを駆使して2回焼成で完成させた作品です。
The patterns of the background were done with Indian ink (p. 48) and blue luster on the mother-of-pearl luster.

※制作方法解説は72〜74頁、下絵は97頁に掲載。
Refer to p. 72-74 how to paint this piece. The line drawing is on p. 97.

暁の蓮　Heavenly Lotus　34.8 × 34.8 cm

ピンクの蓮の花には金盛りを施してビーズ装飾を行いました。
右下の黒っぽい金色の葉は、食品用のラップを使ってテクスチャーを作りました。
Glass beads were applied on the petals of the lotus . The texture of black leaf was done with cling film.

※制作方法解説は75〜77頁、下絵は98頁に掲載。
Refer to p. 75-77 how to paint this piece. The line drawing is on p. 98.

輝きの時　Golden Moment　6.0 × 14.0 × 30.0 cm
金色の蓮の葉はメタリックゴールドを焼き付けた上にオリーブグリーンで影を付けて仕上げています。
The gold leaf was done with metallic gold shaded with Olive Green.

21

22

夕暮れの藤　Evening Wisteria　D 20.8 × 37.0 ㎝

藤の葉はプラチナとマット金を焼き付けた上に絵の具を塗り、食品用ラップを使ってテクスチャーを表現しました。
花瓶の口と脚の部分のマット金の上には真珠ラスターを塗っています。
The texture of the leaves was made with cling film. mother-of-pearl luster was applied on the gold edge.

花の背景の緑色の部分は、焼成後のイエローラスターに水色ラスターを塗り、乾燥後にマーブルローションを塗って焼成しました。白い縁にはホワイトマット（ホワイト、マット粉、エナメルフリット１：１：２）を塗っています。

花の集い　Floral Harmony in a Box　D 17.2 × 37.0 cm

花の背景の緑色の部分は、焼成後のイエローラスターに水色ラスターを塗り、乾燥後にマーブルローションを塗って焼成しました。白い縁にはホワイトマット（ホワイト、マット粉、エナメルフリット１：１：２）を塗っています。

The background of the flower was done with marble lotion applied on yellow luster and blue luster.
The white mat border was done with white mat (white, mat powder, enamel frit 1:1:2).

※99頁に下絵を掲載。
The line drawing is on p. 99.

椿のティーセット　Camellias on Tea Set

角皿 Square plate: 25.0 × 25.0 cm　カップ Cup: 8.0 × 8.0 × 5.2 cm　ソーサー Saucer: 11.0 × 11.0 cm　ポット Pot: 10.0 × 14.5 × 17.2 cm

紅椿の金の花びらと葉はオンゴールドで描き、金の椿の花と葉はメタリックゴールドの下地に描きました。
背景のリボンは、水色ラスターの上に模様のシールを貼り、メタリックホワイトをパディングして仕上げました。
The gold petals and leaves with the red camellia were painted with red brown on gold.
The gold camellia was painted with metallic gold. The blue ribbons were padded with metallic white on blue luster over the stickers.

※99頁に下絵を掲載。　The line drawing is on p. 99.

葉は焼成したマット金の上にレッドブラウンで影を付け、ブラックエナメルでアウトラインを描いています。
背景はマット金を焼き付けた上に真珠ラスターを乗せました。

紫陽花の花束　Hydrangea Bouquet　D 23.0 cm

紫陽花の花びらは、サイズの異なる2種類のガラスビーズで装飾しました。
葉は焼成したマット金の上にレッドブラウンで影を付け、ブラックエナメルでアウトラインを描いています。
背景はマット金を焼き付けた上に真珠ラスターを乗せました。

The hydrangeas were decorated with two different sizes of glass beads.
The gold leaves were painted with Red Brown and black enamel.
The background was done with mother-of-pearl luster on gold.

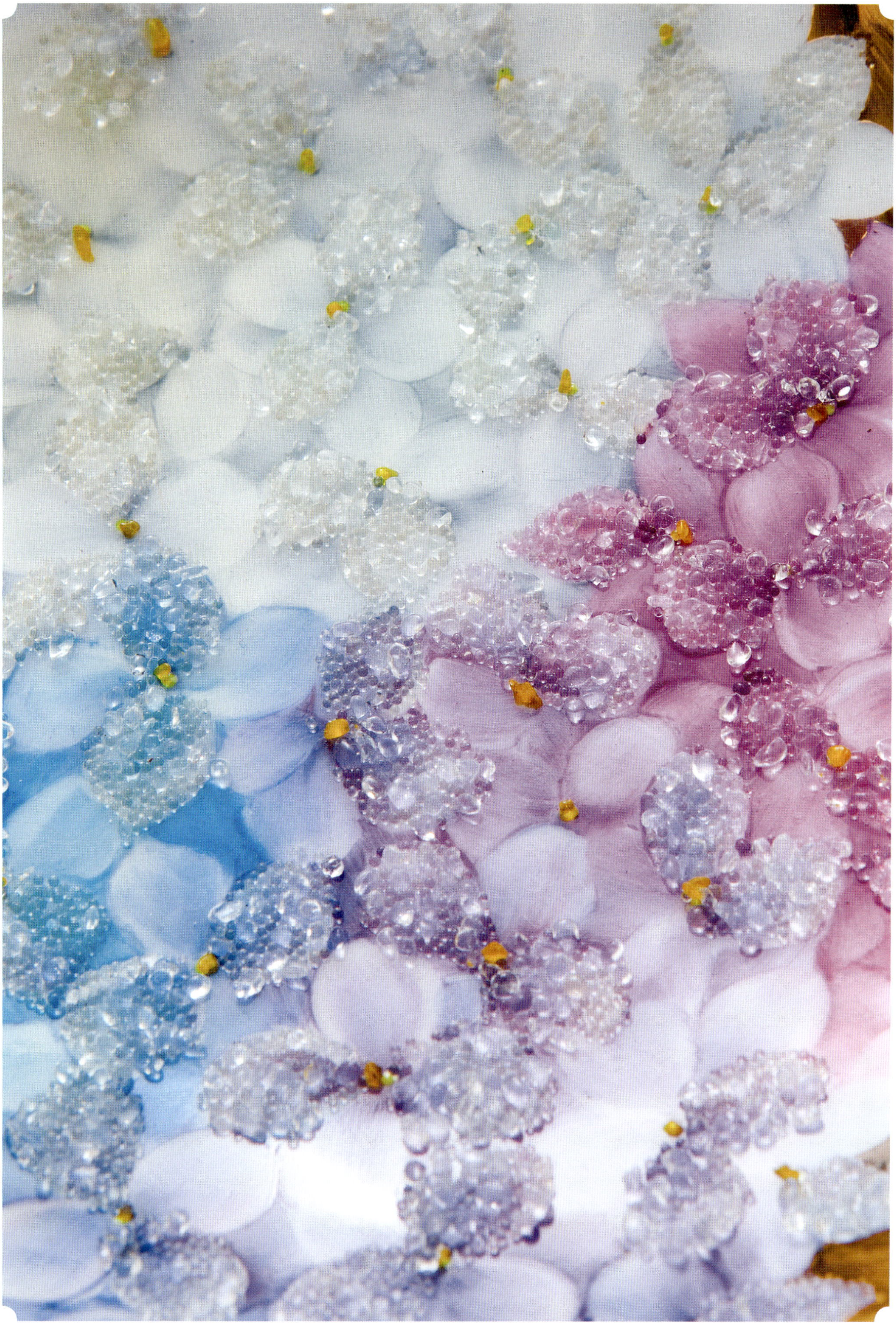

籠の蝶々　Butterflies in a Basket　D 17.2 × 5.0cm

蝶の装飾には3種類のガラスビーズを使っています。
背景は金の地塗りの上にブラックラスターを塗り、さらにマーブルローションを使ってテクスチャーを作りました。
The butterflies were decorated with three different sizes of glass beads.
The background was done with black luster and marble lotion on bright gold.

※100頁に下絵を掲載。
The line drawing is on p. 100.

唐草模様の色はあらかじめ黒地の下にピンクやブルーを焼き付けて、
マスキング液で模様を描き、ブラックをパディングしました。

蝶の宝石　Jeweled Butterfly　11.0 × 15.0 × 5.0 cm

唐草模様の色はあらかじめ黒地の下にピンクやブルーを焼き付けて、
マスキング液で模様を描き、ブラックをパディングしました。

The black background was applied after painting swirl with red resist on fired pink and blue colors.

※100頁に下絵を掲載。
The line drawing is on p. 100.

金の花弁はガラスビーズを高温焼成した結果、チッピングオフでは作ることのできない
ダイナミックな釉薬剥離が起こったので、そこに金を塗りました。

※101頁に下絵を掲載。

牡丹狂乱 Strange-looking Peonies D 22.5 × 6.0 cm

金の花弁はガラスビーズを高温焼成した結果、チッピングオフでは作ることのできない
ダイナミックな釉薬剥離が起こったので、そこに金を塗りました。

The gold petals were made by applying glass beads on them and fired at high temperature to chip off.
Gold was applied on the chipped off area producing a dynamic results.

※101頁に下絵を掲載。
The line drawing is on p. 101.

31

縁の部分は墨はじきで模様を描きました。花びらには丸粒のガラスビーズを焼き付けています。

朝露とクレマチス　Clematis with Dewdrops　D22.8 × 6.0 cm

The pattern of the edge was done with Indian ink as a resist,
followed by blue luster on the mother-of-pearl luster.
The round-shaped glass beads were applied on the petals.

※102頁に下絵を掲載。
The line drawing is on p. 102.

舞扇　Fans for Japanese Dance　D 22.8 × 6.0 cm

背景は焼成したロイヤルバイオレットの上にブラックを塗り、食品用のラップを使ってテクスチャーを作っています。
プラチナの扇の上の椿はローズマロンで描きました。
花芯の部分は焼成したガラス片の上に金で色を付けています。

The texture of the background was done with Black and cling film on the Royal Violet.
The silver fans were painted with Rose Maroon on the mat platinum.
The center of the flower was painted gold on the fired glass lump.

※103頁に下絵を掲載。
The line drawing is on p. 103.

牡丹のコサージュ　Peony Corsage　D 14.2 × 12.8 cm

メタリックホワイトの下地には真珠ラスターが塗ってあるので、白地が上品な輝きを放ちます。

The gentle metallic white glow is due to the mother-of-pearl luster underneath.

更紗牡丹　Chiffon Peonies　D 22.8 × 6.0 cm

下地から花まで全てメタリック絵の具を使って描いています。
This box was painted with metallic paints all over.

睡蓮と鯉　Carp with Water Lilies　陶板 tile 35.0 × 25.0 cm

金の鯉と金の葉は、メタリックゴールドの上にブラック、レッドブラウンで影を入れて描いています。
水中の泡は真珠ラスターの上にピーコックブルーで影を付けました。

The gold carp was painted with Black on metallic gold. The gold leaves were painted with Reddish Brown on metallic gold.
The bubbles were painted with Peacock Blue on mother-of-pearl luster.

2章［テクニック紹介］
Chapter 2　Techniques

ガラスビーズ装飾のアイディアとテクニック
Ideas and techniques with glass-beading

　ガラスビーズを使った磁器装飾は、1990年代に刊行されたJ.V.Patten氏著『Nippon Porcelain』シリーズにおいて、日本の輸出陶磁器に用いられた技法の一つCoralene（コラーレン）として広く紹介されていますので、オールドノリタケに興味をお持ちの方であれば一度は何かの写真でご覧になっていることと思います。また、実際の技法に関しては株式会社サンアート制作、高木春枝氏指導のテキスト『イッチン盛り絵付け』でも具体的に紹介されています。

　私はこれらの書籍を参考に実験を重ね、さらに米国の材料店のアドバイスを受けて、独自の手法でガラスビーズを作品の装飾に応用するようになりました。ここではその技法についてご紹介します。

　コラーレンの伝統的な手法では、あらかじめ色付けしたエナメルを糊代わりにし、白磁に直接、色エナメルを塗ってそこにガラスビーズを付けるので、高度な技の熟練が必要です。一方、私の方法では、まず一般的な絵付け方法で完成させた絵に、ガラスビーズを焼き付けて装飾します。完成した作品があれば、誰でも簡単にその後のガラスビーズ装飾を楽しめるのがこの方法の特徴です。また、透明の糊(エナメルフリットまたはフラッキス)を使い絵の具で表現したグラデーションをそのままガラスに反映することができるので、色エナメルだけでは表現しきれない微妙な色を表現することができます。

The decoration style with glass beads on porcelain was shown in the series of books entitled *Nippon Porcelain* written by J. V. Patten in 1990s. It was called "Coralene" that were exported from Japan to USA as one of styles of Old Noritake. Old Noritake fans may have seen them on the collectors' books. The technical detail had once been shown on the text book *Icchinmori Etsuke* by Harue Takagi edited by Sun-Art about 10 years ago in Japan.

　I learned the technique of "Coralene" from those books and tried them in several manners and finally reached the best way to work with the glass beads as advised by a supplier Gloria Ann McCarthy of USA.

　Let me explain about this "glass-beading" which is different from the manner of "Coralene."

　In the technique of "Coralene", they use tinted white enamel as the glue for glass beads. They put the tinted enamel directly on the unpainted porcelain and then apply the glass beads on the glue. High level skill is required to produce gradation color with the glue. In Hanajima Method, first of all we complete the painting before applying the glass beads on top. In other words, the porcelain looks just a plain finish painted piece before beading. So, if someone has finished pieces, she can do glass-beading on the pieces any time. The gradation colors made by shading with the paints can be shown through the transparent glue (enamel frit) and glass beads.

数年前に描いたライラックの皿。
A simple lilac plate painted few years ago.

ラスターとガラスビーズでリメイク後。中央の部分は全面に丸粒タイプのガラスビーズを敷き詰めるように付けて焼成した。ガラスの中に閉じ込められた花の色の見え方が角度によって変化し、元の作品とはまた別の面白さが生まれた。
The lilac plate was upgraded with luster and glass beads. The lilac was covered with round-shaped glass beads. It shows another face under the lighting.

● **主な材料**

まず主要材料である透明ガラスビーズは、アートフラワーの装飾等で使われている大きさや形の異なるもの3、4種類を作品のプランに応じて使い分けています。これらは手芸・工芸関連の材料店で入手できます。

ガラスを付ける糊代わりには、エナメルフリット（透明盛り）または絵の具の艶出しに使われるフラッキスを遅乾性の調合油（エナメルオイル）で溶いて使用しています。

＊エナメルオイル＝バルサムとミネラルオイルを1：1の割合で混ぜたもの。

The materials

The "glass beads" can be obtained from crafts store being sold as a material for "artificial flower." There are different sizes and shapes. One can choose from any of them according to the decoration plan on the porcelain.

"Enamel frit" or "flax" is the glue for the "glass beads." Enamel or flax is mix with enamel oil made from mixing balsam of copiba and heavy mineral oil 1:1.

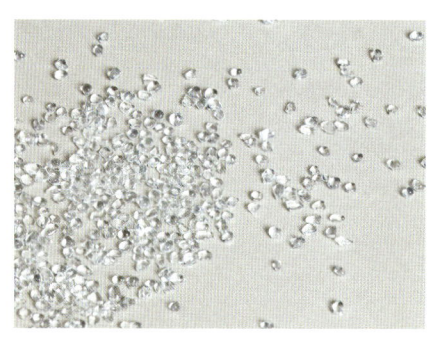

ガラスビーズL（2〜3mm）
Glass beads L (2-3mm)

ガラスビーズM（1mm）
Glass beads M (1mm)

ガラスビーズS（0.5mm）
Glass beads S (0.5mm)

ガラスビーズ丸粒（1mm）。
色味はグレーがかっている。
Round-shaped glass beads (1mm).
They look pale gray.

＊本文中のガラスビーズのS、M、Lサイズは、〈アメリカンフラワーダイヤスビーズ〉（亀島商店）のSS、S、Mサイズに該当します。

［例］**朝露とクレマチス**（32頁）
Clematis with Dewdrops (p. 32)

クレマチスの花弁には丸粒のガラスビーズが添付されている。
The some petals of clematis were covered with round-shaped glass beads.

39

● 作品づくりの手順

土台となる絵付け完成後、ガラスビーズを乗せる部分を特定し、その上にエナメルオイルでマヨネーズ状に練ったエナメルフリットを平筆で塗ります。サイズの小さなビーズを使用する場合には厚さが均等になるようにスポンジでならす場合もあります。糊の厚さにムラがあると添付するガラスビーズの厚さにもムラが出る場合がありますので注意が必要です。

次に、作品がすっぽり入るような大きな箱を用意し、その中に新聞紙などの大きな紙を敷き詰めます。その箱にエナメルフリットを塗った作品を入れ、好みの大きさのガラスビーズを雪が積もるようにたっぷりと振りかけます。

その後、作品を持ち上げて軽く振り、余分なガラスビーズを落とします。意図しない場所に貼り付いてしまったガラスビーズは乾いた面相筆で取り除きます。取り除いたガラスは瓶に戻して再度使用することができます。

● 焼成方法

作品は720℃で焼成してゆっくり冷やし、炉内が室温になってから作品を取り出します。焼成温度は大変重要で740℃以上の高温で焼成するとたいていの場合ガラスが溶けて互いにくっつき、冷却後にひび割れて剥離の原因になります。使用する磁器によっても最適な焼成温度の幅はありますが、平均的には720℃が安全だと思われます。

一度焼成したガラスビーズはその後、それ以上の高温で焼成することはできないので、作品の最終段階で焼成します。どうしても再焼成したい場合は720℃以下で焼成すると、2回程度の焼成には耐えることができます。

● 応用テクニック
◇金盛りや色盛りとの組み合わせ

このガラスビーズ装飾では周囲に金盛りを施してコラーレン風の作品を作ることもできます。その場合には、ガラスを付ける前の段階で、ガラスを乗せたい部分の周囲をエナメルまたはレイズドペーストで囲み、土手を作ります。

The process of glass-beading

After finishing painting, choose the beading area and paint the glue which is prepared enamel frit (mixed with enamel oil, appears like mayonnaise) with a flat brush. When we choose the small size beads, it is best to pad on the glue with sponge. Be careful to make flat application of glue; otherwise, beads will not be lie flat.

Prepare large open box. Put newspaper inside the box. Set the porcelain piece in it. Pour the glass beads, like snow falling on the glue-painted area.

Take out the porcelain piece and turn it upside down to expel the unattached beads. Clean off the extra beads on the porcelain with dry brush.

As we can use the extra beads again in the next trial, return them into the original bottle.

The firing of glass-beading

Fire the porcelain at 720℃ (cone 018). Take it out from the kiln after the temperature had cooled down to room temperature.

It is important not to fire over 720℃. If the firing temperature is over 740℃, the glass beads melt and fused together. It is possible that after cooling down crack may occur. Although the best temperature is different according to the quality of the porcelain, 720℃ is always safe for the glass beads.

Glass beads should be fired at the last firing as they cannot stand high temperature over 720℃. However, the glass beads can be fired twice under the 720℃.

The applications with glass-beading
The combination with raised gold and raised enamel

Raised gold can be applied on the edge of the beading area similar to "Coralene." This is possible by applying yellow enamel or raised

[例] 花の集い（24頁）　Floral Harmony in a Box (p. 24)

花びらをガラスビーズで装飾している。
Some of the petals were decorated with glass beads.

[例] 籠の蝶々（28頁）　Butterflies in a Basket (p. 28)

蝶の羽には大きさの異なるガラスビーズを組み合わせている。
The butterfly was decorated with glass beads in three different sizes.

焼成後、金またはプラチナで土手に色付けし再度焼成します。その後ガラスビーズを付けたい部分にエナメルフリットを塗り、同様にガラスビーズを付けて焼成します。ひと手間かけることで、よりきらびやかな装飾を楽しむことができます。

エナメルの土手を色盛りで表現する場合もあります。黒エナメル、白エナメルなども工夫次第で、ガラスと融合して面白い表現ができます。

◇色付きガラスビーズの使用

このガラスビーズの装飾方法の特徴は、透明なガラスビーズと透明な糊（エナメルフリット）を使うことで、土台のグラデーションをより効果的に際立たせることです。ピンクやブルーの色付きの透明ガラスビーズを使う場合には下地に色を付けずに、白磁に直接ガラスビーズを焼き付けてガラスの色そのものを楽しむような作品にする方が効果的です。

● 注意点とトラブル対処法

ガラスビーズは摩擦によって剥離しやすいので、作品を梱包する際には注意が必要です。また、糊として鉛分を含む絵の具をたくさん使うので、食器ではなく装飾品のみに使用し、楽しんで下さい。

ガラスビーズ装飾の過程で、私の教室の生徒さん達に起こった問題点とその対処法などを、下記にまとめましたので参考にして下さい。

焼成後、作品を家に持ち帰ったらほとんどのガラスビーズが剥離していた。
▶ ビーズを付ける時、糊の量が少なすぎたのが原因でした。残りのビーズを全て、へらで剥がし、下地と同じ色の糊を作り、再度ガラスビーズを付けて720℃で焼成し修正しました。

作品を箱に入れて持ち運んだ際にガラスビーズが部分的に剥離してしまった。
▶ 剥離した部分に下地と同じ色の糊を塗ってビーズを付け、720℃で再焼成して修正しました。

うっかり760℃以上で焼成したら、ガラスビーズに亀裂が入ってしまった。
▶ ガラスビーズの上にチッピングオフを塗り、再び780℃で焼成してガラスを完全に剥がしてから、そこに金やプラチナを塗り、異なるテクスチャーにしました。

または、剥がした後に再び絵の具を塗って焼成し、ガラスビーズを再び付けて720℃で焼成することでも修正できます。この方法はガラスビーズをしっかりと付着させたい場合に応用できます。磁器をあらかじめチッピングオフして剥がし、その部分に色塗りし、焼成後そこにガラスビーズを付けることで、強く定着させることができます。

paste on the edge before beading. After firing, gold or platinum is painted over it and fired. This is followed with glass-beading application as previously explained. The gold makes nice accent with the glass beads.

We can apply black enamel or white enamel instead of raised gold; they add special charm on the pieces.

Applying colored glass beads

The merit of this "glass-beading" is that the paint colors can be shown through the transparent glue and transparent glass beads. If you try to use colored beads like pink or blue, it is better not to do porcelain painting under the beads. Just put them directly on the white porcelain to let the glass colors be seen.

Cautions and trouble-shooting

As the glass beads come out easily with friction, wrap carefully when you put the piece into the box.

Also, as the enamel frit contains lead, it is better to use the glass beads only for decorative purposes and not for table wares.

On the process of teaching this technique, students have some problems with this beading. So, the followings are FAQ for your reference.

Q: Most of the beads dropped off from the porcelain after the firing. What causes it?
A: It could be because of insufficient amount of the glue was applied. Remove all the glass beads and paint again and apply enough glue to do the glass-beading.

Q: Some of the glass beads dropped off when transporting. How do you repair?
A: Apply tinted glue on the space left by the fallen beads, put back the beads and fire at 720℃ (cone 018) again.

Q: Glass beads were fired with hot temperature over 760℃ (cone 017) by mistake and the beads had crack on it. How do you repair?
A: Remove the all glass beads with chip off powder by firing again at 780℃ (cone 016). Put gold or platinum on the texture.
Another idea is to paint it again and put the glass beads again and fire at 720℃.
This failure leads to new idea, for instance, if we wish glass beads to bind strongly to the porcelain chip off the glaze before glass-beading and beads will bind strongly on the rough surface of the porcelain.

● ガラスビーズ装飾の基本

ガラスビーズを使った基本的な装飾方法について説明します。このテクニックでは金盛りは必ずしも必要ではありませんが、ガラスビーズとの対比で華やかなアクセントになる場合もあります。ここでは金盛り部分も含めて説明します。

初めに、通常の手法で磁器に絵を描き焼成します。この完成作品が土台になります。描く際にグラデーションのメリハリをはっきり付けると、後に添付するガラスビーズがより美しく映えます。

この例では、金盛りの土台には乾燥を待たずに焼成できるイエローエナメルを使っています。レイズドペーストを使うこともできますが、その際には完全乾燥後に焼成して下さい。

ガラスビーズ用の糊としてエナメルフリットを使っていますが、フラッキスで代用することもできます。

The basic of the glass-beading

In this paragraph, I am going to show my own technique how to apply the glass beads on the porcelain, and the raised gold around the glass beads. The raised gold is not always necessary to accompany glass beads. However, it will be pretty accent to decorate glass beads.

First of all, finish painting the motif on the porcelain. Then this finished motif will be the base of the glass beads. If you can create strong contrasting colors on the motif, glass beads will look more dynamic.

Yellow enamel is used as the base of raised gold in this technique, as it can be fire before it is dry.

In case you use raised paste as the base of raised gold, you have to dry it before firing.

Flax can be glue for the glass beads instead of enamel frit.

[例] 蓮の小皿　※104頁に下絵を掲載。
Lotus　The line drawing is on p. 104.

1 蓮の絵を描いて焼成した状態。
A lotus is painted on the plate.

2 エナメルフリットとイエロー絵の具（7：3）をエナメルオイルで溶き、イエローエナメルを作る。
Make yellow enamel by mixing enamel frit and yellow 7:3.

3 イエローエナメルを花弁の縁に土手状に盛り、780℃で焼成する。
Apply yellow enamel on the outline of the petals. Fire at 780℃ (cone 016).

4 イエローエナメルの上にマット金を塗る。
Apply mat gold on the yellow enamel.

5 760℃で焼成する。
Fire at 760℃ (cone 017).

6 エナメルフリットをエナメルオイルでマヨネーズ状に溶き糊を作る。
Mix enamel frit with enamel oil to make glue for glass beads.

7 ビーズを付けたい部分に溶いたエナメルフリットを塗る。
Paint the enamel frit on your favorite petals.

8 糊を付けた作品を紙を敷き詰めた箱の中に入れる。
Put the plate into a paper-lined box.

9 Mサイズのガラスビーズをたっぷりと振りかける。
Pour gently glass beads M on the plate like snow falling.

10 皿を裏返し、余分なビーズを落とす。
Turn the plate upside down to remove the un-attached glass beads.

11 金盛りの上に付着した不要なビーズを筆で取り除く。
Remove gently the extra beads with dry brush.

12 720℃で焼成して完成。焼成によりエナメルフリットの白が透明に変化するので、下地の絵の具の色がきれいに出る。
Fire at 720℃ (cone 018) to complete. The paint color shows as the color of the enamel frit changed from white to transparent.

● いろいろな大きさのビーズを分けて付ける

　大きさの異なるガラスビーズ（S、M、L）を部分ごとに分けて付ける方法を説明します。下の例では、数年前に描いたパンジーの皿をガラスビーズ装飾でリメイクしました。花弁や葉はブラックエナメルで縁取りしてあります。小さいサイズのガラスビーズから順に基本作業を繰り返します。

Apply glass beads of different sizes on separated places

The pansy plate painted few years ago will be decorated with three different sizes of glass beads S, M and L. The petals and leaves are outlined with black enamel. Start beading from the small size beads step by step.

[例] パンジーの皿
Blooming Pansy

1 数年前に描いたパンジーの皿をガラスビーズ装飾でリメイクする。
A pansy plate painted few years ago is decorated with glass beads.

2 Sサイズのビーズを付けたい部分に糊を塗り、ビーズを付ける。
Apply glue and glass beads S on the leaves.

3 Mサイズのビーズを付けたい部分に糊を塗り、ビーズを付ける。
Apply glue and glass beads M on the petals.

4 Lサイズのビーズを付けたい場所に糊を塗り、ビーズを付ける。
Apply glue and glass beads L on the petals.

5 720℃で焼成して完成。
Fire at 720℃ (cone 018) to complete.

◉ いろいろな大きさのビーズを混ぜて付ける

大きさの異なるガラスビーズを混ぜて付ける方法を説明します。下の例では花弁に縁取りはしてありません。大きいサイズのビーズから順に作業を進めます。

[例] 紫陽花の皿
Hydrangea Bouquet

Apply glass beads M and L on the same place

We show how to apply glass beads M and L together on the same place. We have no outline on the petals. Start beading from the large size beads.

1 焼成後の紫陽花の皿。さらに華やかなアクセントを付けるため、花弁にLとM、2種類のガラスビーズを混ぜて焼き付ける。

The firing result of the hydrangea plate. We are going to apply glass beads M and L to add brilliant accent on the petals.

2 ビーズを付ける花弁全部に糊を塗り、必要量のLサイズのビーズを手に取り、ランダムに振りかける。

Apply glue on all the petals to be beaded. Apply glass beads L on the glue randomly.

3 Lサイズのビーズを付け終えた状態。あちこちにランダムなスペースが残っている。

We still have some spaces on the petals.

4 Mサイズのビーズを、スペースを埋めるようにたっぷりと振りかけ、余分なガラスを落とす。

Apply enough glass beads M on the spaces. Remove the extra beads.

5 720℃で焼成して完成。

Fire at 720℃ (cone 018) to complete.

45

ラスターを使ったアイディアとテクニック
Ideas and techniques with luster

● **ラスターの不思議**

ラスターは使うほどに奥が深く、やっと馴染んだかと思うとふとした拍子に気まぐれで裏切られるような、私にとっては小悪魔のような不思議な絵付け材料です。ラスター油を使った希釈の程度や磁器の色によっても発色が異なるので、毎回同じ色を出すことは難しく、いつも一回勝負にかけるような気持ちでラスターと向き合っています。

しかしこうしてラスターと根気よく付き合っているうちに、意外な材料との相性の良さや、柔軟性にも気が付くようになってきました。本書では、そうしたラスターのコンビネーションテクニックを使った作品をご紹介していますが、そのポイントを下記にまとめましたので作品鑑賞の参考になさって下さい。

● **ラスターとイングレーズ絵の具**

イングレーズテクニックで適切に焼成された場合、絵の具は完全に釉薬の中に浸透し、磁器の表面はなめらかな状態に仕上がります。ですからその上にラスターを塗った場合、色ガラスを重ねたような深みのある光沢を得ることができます。両者の間には「透明な釉薬」が存在するので、混色による色の混濁もありません。ラスター同士、イングレーズ絵の具同士では混色が困難な色を様々に組み合わせることもできます。

● **ラスターの重ね塗り**

ラスターは焼成後に異なる色を重ねて塗ることもできます。その際に上下の色が互いに反応して色変しますので、必ず焼成実験をして相性の良い色同士を組み合わせて下さい。

真珠ラスターはブルー系や赤紫系のラスターと大変相性が良いので、私は多くの作品に応用しています。

Mystical luster
Luster is mystical. Using luster is full of amazing surprises, but difficult to handle. Luster gives us surprising results, unexpectedly after firing. Luster looks different depending on the amount applied, on the luster thinner ratio and the quality of the porcelain glaze. That's why luster work is a kind of a gamble for us. In using luster, some of the combination ideas with other paints were produced by chances. You can see those results on my pieces; hopefully these may help you with your understanding of luster techniques.

Luster on in-glaze paints
The painting result of the in-glaze painting is smooth on the surface as the paints sink into the glaze completely. With double coats of luster painted and in-glaze paint, the piece will look brilliant. As we have the glaze like a sandwich between luster and paint, they never get a muddy look. That's why we can try several combinations with luster colors and in-glaze colors.

The double coats with lusters
The double coat can be done with different luster colors. The color changes after second firing as they affect each other. It is important to test the color combination on the planning of the design. The mother-of-pearl luster can make nice harmony with blue or red luster, the results are shown on my pieces.

[例] **睡蓮と鯉** (36頁)

Carp with Water Lilies (p. 36)

鯉の影は、真珠ラスターの上にブルーマザーオブパールラスターを重ねて表現しています。
The shadow of the carp was done with double coat of mother-of-pearl luster and blue mother-of-pearl luster.

● ラスターと金の組み合わせ

焼成後のマット金に真珠ラスターを塗ることで金属的なレインボーカラーのマーブルを表現することができます。この手法は大変魅力的で、私は様々な作品に応用しています。

The combination with luster and gold
We can get metallic rainbow marble colors by applying mother-of-pearl luster on the fired gold. As this texture is so charming, they are used on my pieces.

[例] 四季の舞扇 (8頁)
Four Seasons (p. 8)

扇の骨は、金のみで描いた部分と、金の上に真珠ラスターを重ねた部分を交互に配置しています。
The hinge area was painted with mat gold and mother-of-pearl luster and vice-versa.

● ラスターとメタリック絵の具の組み合わせ

通常の絵の具はラスターの上に重ねることで、化学変化が起こり色が変わることがあります。メタリック絵の具はラスターの影響を受けませんが、下地の色によって見え方が変わります。

The combination with luster and metallic paints
Although some of the regular paints change color when they are applied on the luster because of the chemical effect after firing, metallic paints do not change.

[例] 暁の蓮 (20頁)
Heavenly Lotus (p. 20)

真珠ラスターの上にメタリックホワイトを乗せたので、白く見える。
Metallic white was painted on the mother-of-pearl luster, which looks white.

水色ラスターの上にメタリックホワイトを乗せたので、銀色に見える。
Metallic white was painted on the blue luster, which looks silver.

47

● ラスターの墨はじき

剥がす必要のないラスターのマスキングとしては、すでにカットブルーがあり広く便利に使われていますが、墨汁を同様の用途に使うこともできます。ここでは墨ならではのテクニックをご紹介します。

カットブルーに比べて粘度の低い墨汁は、細い線や繊細な表現が可能です。下の例のように、墨汁をペンに付けてラスターのマスキングとしてペン描き模様を描いたり、墨汁で塗った面を乾いた直後にスクラッチしてラスターの線描き模様を表現することもできます。

墨を使う際の注意点は次の通りです。

○濃い墨が使いやすいので、上澄みを使わないように、必ず使用前に墨汁の容器を振って液の濃度を調整する。
○墨は鉛筆やカーボンをはじくので、下描きすることはできない。
○下地に墨が乗らない場合があるので下地を膠液または微量のバルサムであらかじめ拭いておくと失敗がない。
○焼成後は、アルコールでしっかり拭くことによって、墨で描いた絵柄がはっきり現れる。

Masking with Indian ink

We have "cut blue" as a masking liquid for the luster. This is useful as we have no need to remove it before firing. Indian ink for Japanese calligraphy can be used for the same purpose. Indian ink has also another capability with luster. The following ideas are the luster technique which can be done only with the Indian ink. We can draw the fine line with Indian ink as it is more fluid than cut blue. We can do pen work and draw some pattern as a resist on luster. We also can scratch on the painting surface of Indian ink to make fine line over luster.

When you use Indian ink, be sure to shake well the bottle before using.

We cannot use waxed carbon paper to trace the pattern for Indian ink as the ink is water-based, which is not compatible with wax.

A kind of glue "nikawa" or a drop of the balsam of copaiba can make a nice base coat for Indian ink.

After firing, we have to clean the soil remains of Indian ink on porcelain with alcohol to get clear texture.

[例] 墨はじきを応用したミニ・クリスマスプレート
A small Christmas plate painted with Indian ink

1 ペンで模様を描き、一部を筆で塗りつぶす。
Pen the pattern and paint some parts with Indian ink.

2 ペンで文字を描くこともできる。
We can pen the characters.

3 塗りつぶした部分が乾くのを待ち、スクラッチして模様を描く。
Just after the ink is dried, scratch the pattern on it.

4 ドライヤーで完全に乾かす。
Dry completely with dryer.

5 赤色ラスターを皿全面に塗る。
Paint red luster all over the plate.

6 ラスターを塗った皿を780℃で焼成する。
Fire it at 780℃ (cone 016).

7 焼成直後。模様がよくわからない状態。
Just after firing, the pattern made with Indian ink cannot be recognized.

8 アルコールでしっかりと拭くことによって墨で描いた模様が現れる。
After wiping completely with some force with the alcohol, the pattern appears on the plate.

9 完成。好みで装飾のドットなどを加えても面白い。
The firing result. Enamel dots may produce a charming plate.

作例で使用した墨汁
I used Indian ink for this technique.

49

メタリック絵の具のアイディアとテクニック
Ideas and techniques with metallic paints

● メタリック絵の具と上絵の具の組み合わせ

メタリック絵の具を使うにはいくつかの方法がありますが、私は作品の装飾目的や同時に使う溶剤との兼ね合いによってその方法を変えています。

下地塗りの場合には、通常の絵の具よりもゆるめに溶きます。オイルは、バルサムとミネラルオイルを1：2の割合で調合したオイル（調合油）、または水溶性のスクラッチリキッドを使います。調合油の場合には筆で下地塗りしてからスポンジでパディングしますが、スポンジ跡が付く場合があります。スクラッチリキッドを使う場合には、絵の具をたらした時しずくが流れて切れないくらいにトロトロに溶いて、直接スポンジで塗布します。この加減はメタリック絵の具を使いスクラッチテクニックを行う場合と同じです。絵の具の濃度が濃い場合には厚塗りになり、剥離の原因になります。

メタリック絵の具は盛りに使うこともできます。特に金色や銀色のメタリック絵の具はエナメルフリットと半々の割合でエナメルオイル（バルサムとミネラルオイル1：1）で溶き、金盛りのような使い方をすることができます。この方法は1回焼成で金盛りや銀盛り風のテクスチャーを作ることができるので、大変便利です。

Combination with paints

There are several ways to apply metallic paints on porcelain. The medium should be chosen according to the situation on the process.

In the process of the wet grounding, the procedure is as follows:

Mixing oil is made with heavy balsam of copaiba and heavy mineral oil 1:2, or scratch liquid can be used. When metallic paint is prepared with mixing oil, paint it with a brush and pad on it with sponge, which may leave sponge texture on it sometimes. In the case with scratch liquid, the consistency should be sauce-like and pad it with sponge directly on the porcelain. This is the same way as in the process of scratch technique. If the paint is too thick, the paint will crack.

Metallic paints can be painted on regular paint or painted under regular paint. The combinations produce a gentle shine on porcelain.

Metallic paints can be used with enamel frit to make raised fake gold and raised fake silver. Mix enamel frit with metallic gold 1:1 with enamel oil (balsam of copaiba and mineral oil 1:1). This is very useful to create raised fake gold or raised fake silver at one firing.

メタリック絵の具
Metallic paints

花芯はエナメルフリットとメタリックゴールド（1：1）を混ぜたゴールドエナメルで表現。
The pollen was created using gold enamel (enamel frit and metallic gold 1:1)

花びらは下地にメタリックゴールドを焼き付け、その上にバイオレットオブアイアンで影を付けた。
The petals were painted with metallic gold, fired and overlaid with violet of iron.

マスキングテープを碁盤の目にカットして、あいた部分にメタリックゴールドをパディングした。
This leaf was painted with metallic gold after masking with square tape on the black base.

ブラックの下地にメタリックゴールドを塗布してスクラッチし、麻の葉模様と唐草模様を描いた。
These leaves were done with scratching metallic gold on the black base.

[例] 花園の鶴（12頁） Celestial Cranes (p. 12)

葉はメタリック絵の具を使い下記の方法で描いた。左の蒔絵風の部分は53頁参照。
The leaves were painted with metallic paints as below. Refer to p.53 how to apply gold relief on the left of the plate.

メタリックシルバーを焼き付け、その上にピーコックブルーで影を入れた。
Apply shadow with peacock blue on the metallic silver.

ピーコックブルーを焼き付け、その上にメタリックシルバーで影を入れた。
Apply shadow with metallic silver on the peacock blue.

メタリックシルバーを焼き付け、その上にルビーブロンズ（メタリック絵の具）で影を入れた。
Apply shadow with Ruby Bronze (metallic paint) on metallic silver.

メタリックゴールドを焼き付け、その上にルビーブロンズ（メタリック絵の具）で影を入れた。
Apply shadow with Ruby Bronze on metallic gold.

クロムグリーンを焼き付け、その上にメタリックゴールドで影を入れた。
Apply shadow with metallic gold on chrome green.

● 無色ラスターとメタリック絵の具の組み合わせ

無色ラスターはあらゆるメタリック絵の具の下地として使うことができます。色を主張せずにつつましい光沢を放ち、しかも絵の具が乗りやすい下地を作ってくれるので、メタリック絵の具の地塗りをする場合には、ひと手間かけてあらかじめ磁器に無色ラスターを塗り焼成しておくとよいでしょう。それにより、メタリック絵の具をなめらかに仕上げ、光沢を引き立てることができます。

The combination with white luster

White luster can be used under the metallic paints as base coat. White luster has a gentle shine and also supports metallic paints to fit nicely on the porcelain.

Apply white luster and fire before applying metallic paints if you need nice grounding on the porcelain. Then you can get smooth texture and brilliance with metallic paints.

[例] 更紗牡丹（35頁） Chiffon Peonies (p. 35)

ボックスの下地になっているメタリックホワイトの下に無色ラスターが焼成してあるので、重ね塗りしているメタリック絵の具の全てが上品な光沢を放っている。また、メタリックゴールドとメタリックシルバーをそれぞれエナメルフリットと混ぜて、金盛り風、銀盛り風に仕上げた。

The base coat of the box of "Chiffon Peonies" was done with white luster which supports all the metallic paints to glow on the box.

The fake raised gold and the fake raised silver are outlined on the petals.

メタリックゴールドの金盛り風 — The fake raised gold
メタリックシルバーの銀盛り風 — The fake raised silver

51

● メタリックゴールドの上に絵の具で描く

メタリックゴールドで下地を作り、上絵の具で絵を描きました。金の光沢が絵の具に映え、金箔画のような独特の雰囲気を醸し出します。

Painting on metallic gold texture
The camellia was painted with regular paints on metallic gold texture. It looks painting on gold leaf.

[例] 椿のボックス
Gold and Camellia

※104頁に下絵を掲載。
The line drawing is on p. 104.

1 下地にメタリックゴールドを焼き付け、下絵をトレースする。
Apply metallic gold with wet grounding. After firing trace the pattern.

2 葉と枝を描いてから、花芯、花弁の順に花を描く。
Start with leaves and branches. Next paint flower.

3 ホワイトエナメル（エナメルフリット、ホワイト1：1）の白盛りで花粉を盛り、780℃で焼成。
Put white enamel as pollen and fire at 780℃ (cone 016).

4 焼成後、黒い帯状の模様を写す。
Trace the pattern.

5 花弁をブラックで描く。
Paint the petals with Black.

6 葉とドットにはブラックエナメル（エナメルフリットとブラック1：1）を盛り、780℃で焼成。
Apply black enamel as the leaves and dots and fire at 780℃ (cone 016).

● メタリックゴールドによる蒔絵風のテクスチャー

下地にブラックを焼き付けた上に、メタリックゴールドを使い蒔絵風の模様を描きました。

黒地に下描きする場合、赤のマジックペンで描くか、または白のカーボン紙で図柄を転写することができます。ただし、白のカーボン紙はカーボンが焼け残る場合がありますので、線を完全に絵の具で覆うことが必要です。

The gold enamel work looks like lacquer work

The black basecoat was done with black paint and fired. The painting was done with metallic gold.

The tracing was done with white carbon paper. As the line may remain on the black coating, be sure to cover all the line with the paints. You may also use red magic pen to draw the line drawing.

[例] **蒔絵風のボックス**
Raised Metallic Gold on Black Box

※104頁に下絵を掲載。
The line drawing is on p. 104.

1 ブラックで地塗りし焼成したら、その上に絵柄をトレースする。
Trace the pattern on the black base.

2 絵柄の周囲を赤のマスキング液でマスキングする。
Apply red resist outside of the pattern.

3 メタリックゴールドをスクラッチリキッドで溶いて絵柄に粗くパディングし、ドライヤーで乾かす。
Apply metallic gold mixed with scratch liquid with sponge of the rim.

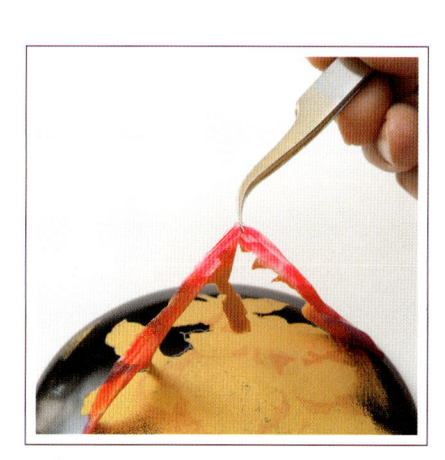

4 マスキングを剥がす。
Remove the red resist.

5 メタリックゴールドとエナメルフリットを1:1の割合でエナメルオイルで溶く。
Mix enamel frit and metallic gold 1:1 with enamel oil.

6 模様の輪郭にアクセントラインのように盛りを施し、点も盛りで描く。
Apply gold enamel as the dots and the accent line of the pattern.

53

イリデッセント絵の具のアイディアとテクニック
Ideas and techniques with iridescent paints

イリデッセント絵の具は焼成後の発色がメタリック絵の具に似ていますが、性質は異なります。まず、焼成前の段階では絵の具の色が白く、ブラックなど濃い下地に描くことで初めて発色するのが特徴です。また、単一の発色になりがちなメタリック絵の具に比べ、イリデッセント絵の具では美しいグラデーションが作れるので、絵画的な表現が可能です。

Iridescent paints
Although the result of the iridescent paints looks similar as that of the metallic paints, they are different in their character.

All the iridescent paints look white before painting. They produce their colors on the dark base. As they can make gradation, picturesque representation can be made more easily with them.

［例］イリデッセントの椿
Iridescent Camellia

下地にブラックを焼き付け、イリデッセント絵の具で影付けを行うように絵を描く。
Paint iridescent paints as shading on black base.

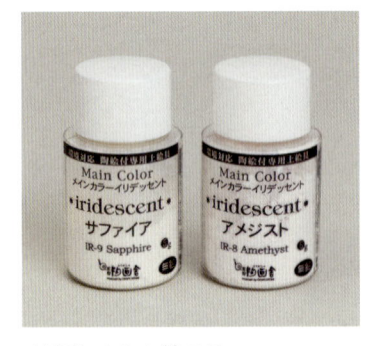

イリデッセント絵の具
Iridescent paints

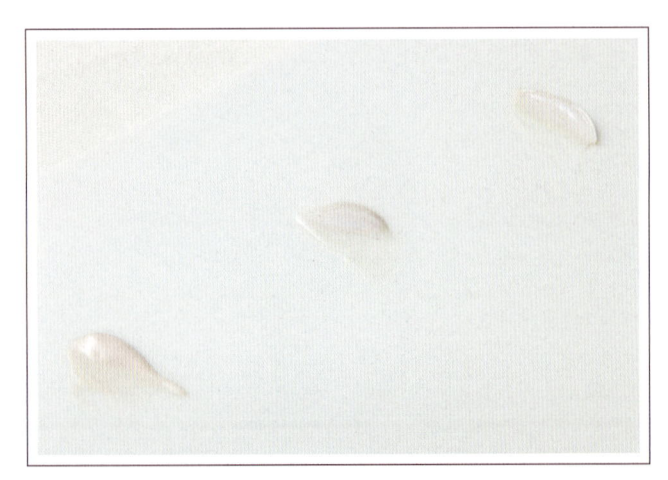

イリデッセント絵の具3色を溶いた状態。左からルビー、サファイア、アメジスト。描く前には色の違いはほとんどない。
From the left, Ruby, Sapphire and Amethyst. The paints look similar.

暗色の下地に描くことで、それぞれの色に発色する。
They produce their colors on the dark base.

イリデッセント絵の具は黒地以外の色の上に使うこともできます。ラスターとは一味違う厚みのある金属的な光沢が表現できます。

Iridescent paints can be painted on the regular paints.

[例] イリデッセントの紫陽花
Iridescent Hydrangea

紫陽花の花を描き完成させる。
Paint hydrangea.

上の作品の花びらと葉に同色系のイリデッセント絵の具、ルビー（濃いピンク）、サファイア（ブルー）、アメジスト（紫）、ペリドット（明るいグリーン）をそれぞれ重ね塗りし780℃で焼成した後、ゴールドエナメルで縁取りした。縁の黒地の上にはホワイトエナメルでドット模様を入れた。
Paint on the petals and leaves with similar iridescent paints. Ruby, Sapphire and Amethyst are on the petals. Peridot is on the leaves. Fire at 780℃ (cone 016). Do the outline of the petals and leaves with gold enamel. Apply white enamel on the black edge.

※106頁に下絵を掲載。
The line drawing is on p. 106.

イングレーズの応用
Applications of in-glaze painting

● イングレーズの基本

　イングレーズ絵の具を使った基本的な絵付け手法は既刊の『ポーセリン・アートの装飾技法』で詳しく説明しておりますので、ここでは簡単にご紹介します。

　イングレーズの技法は専用絵の具を使って磁器の上に描き、1,220℃前後の高温（磁器の種類によって最適温度には多少の幅がある）で焼成することで絵の具が釉薬の中に浸透し、下絵付け風に仕上がる上絵技法の一つです。イングレーズ絵の具は通常の絵の具より、多少もったりして伸びが劣りますが、高温に耐性があります。焼成中の絵の具の飛散を考慮して絵の具を20％程度多めに乗せて描くということが描く上でのコツの一つです。

　焼成後イングレーズ絵の具は釉薬の中に完全に浸透するので、絵の具の溶出がありません。そのため、食器としての用途を考えると大変安全だといえます。

[例] 単色で描いたイングレーズの皿
The monochrome plates painted with in-glaze paints

※3点とも105頁に下絵を掲載。
The line drawings are on p. 105.

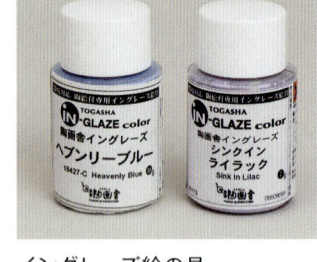

The basic of the in-glaze technique
Introduction and basic explanation of in-glaze painting was covered in one of the chapters of my previous book *Eclectic Sense of East-West Porcelain Art decoration*. This time the explanation will be brief only to highlight some outstanding feature.

　The method is painting in-glaze colors on glazed wares and then fired at 1,220℃ (cone 7). It should be noted that only porcelain suited to this high temperature should be used. On firing, in-glaze colors sink under the glaze and will appear after firing just like under glaze painted porcelain. In using in-glaze colors, it is important to apply 20% more paints than usual because 20% of the paint is lost during firing.

　In-glaze painting is very safe for table wares as the paints sink into the glaze completely and will not contact the food.

イングレーズ絵の具
In-glaze paints

ワイルドローズ：アガットブルー
Wild Rose : Agate Blue

マーガレット：ライトブルー
Marguerite : Light Blue

芍薬：コバルトブルー
Peony : Cobalt Blue

現在では基本24色以上の色が市販されておりイングレーズ絵の具のみでも多様な色の表現が可能になりました。特にブルー系の色には、上絵付け用の絵の具では表現しきれない艶と発色があるので、私は積極的に作品に使っています。

通常の絵の具同様にイングレーズ絵の具を用いてペン描きや、スクラッチテクニックを行うこともできます。

As we can get more than 24 in-glaze colors from the supply stores, we can make several representations using all the in-glaze paints. Especially blue in-glaze paints are excellent because of their brilliance and the depth of the colors on the porcelain. That is the reason why I have many painted blue pieces.

The pen work and the scratch technique can be done on in-glaze paints the same manner as with regular paints.

◇ イングレーズのスクラッチテクニック
Scratching with in-glaze paints

1 イングレーズ絵の具をスクラッチリキッドで中濃ソース程度にゆるく溶く。
Mix in-glaze paint with scratch liquid like sauce.

2 溶いた絵の具をスポンジでパディングし、ドライヤーで完全に乾かす。
Pad the paint on the piece with sponge. Dry it completely with dryer.

3 スクラッチスティックで模様を描く。絵の具の粉は柔らかい乾いた筆で取り除く。
Scratch the pattern and remove the powder paint with soft dry brush.

◇ イングレーズのペン描き
Penning with in-glaze paints

通常の絵の具同様にイングレーズ絵の具をペンオイルで溶いてペン描きすることができる。
Pen work with in-glaze paints. In-glaze paints can be penned with pen oil as regular paints.

17頁の作品の縁文様にはイングレーズのスクラッチテクニックとペン描きを応用している（78〜79頁参照）。
The border design of the piece on p. 17 was done with penning and scratching. Refer to p. 78-79.

57

● 呉須で描くイングレーズ

呉須（下絵付け用絵の具）を使ってイングレーズ作品を描くことができます。絵付け材料店で入手できるペースト状に練られた水溶性の呉須または粉状の呉須を遅乾性の水溶性メディウムでゆるめに溶き、上絵付けと同様の方法で描きます。イングレーズ絵の具と同様に1,220℃で焼成することにより、呉須が釉薬に浸み込み下絵付け風の作品が完成します。

Paint on glaze with *gosu*

We can use *gosu* (under-glaze paints) instead of in-glaze paints. The paints are sold as paste or powder at the supply store. We can mix it with water-based, slow-drying medium. Paint it on the piece with the same painting way as regular paints. The firing temperature is 1,220℃ (cone 7) which is the same as regular in-glaze painting. Since the paint will sink underneath the glaze, the fired piece will look like under-glaze painted.

[例] **呉須で描くバラ**
Roses done with *gosu*

ペースト状の呉須を使って描いたイングレーズ作品。
This plate was done with *gosu* the same way painting with in-glaze paint.

※106頁に下絵を掲載。
The line drawing is on p. 106.

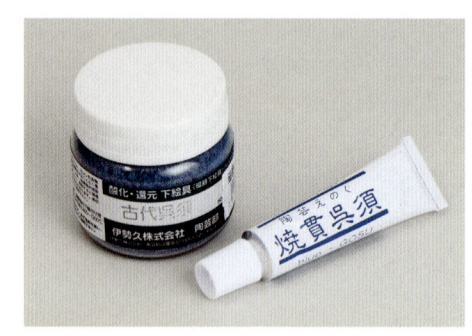

呉須
Gosu (under-glaze paints)

1 呉須を、遅乾性水溶性メディウムでマヨネーズ程度の濃度に溶く。
Mix *gosu* with water-based medium (slow dry type) like mayonnaise.

2 平筆を使い、通常の方法と同様に描く。これを1,220℃で焼成すると、呉須の色はブルーに変わる。
Paint the same way as painting with in-glaze painting with a flat brush. Fire at 1,220℃ (cone 7).

● イングレーズとラスター

　焼成後のイングレーズにラスターを組み合わせ、磁器の輝きをさらに際立たせるテクニックがあります。

　イングレーズで描いた作品の特徴は絵の具が完全に釉薬の中に浸み込んでいるので表面は白磁のようにつるつるに仕上がることです。ですからその上に、白磁に描くように上絵の具を重ねることもできますし、ラスターも光沢を失わずにきれいに乗せることができます。上に乗せたラスターの色と土台のイングレーズの色が融合し、深い味わいのある色になります。

　たとえばブルーイングレーズの上に水色ラスターを乗せることでイングレーズ絵の具またはラスター単独では表現しきれない深いブルーを表現することができます。ブルーイングレーズと真珠ラスター、ブルーイングレーズと水色ラスターは特に相性の良い組み合わせとして私の作品でもさまざまな形で応用しています。

　イングレーズの焼成は大変高温なので、上絵付けとの組み合わせをする場合、必ず最初に焼成を行います。

In-glaze painting with luster

The combination of in-glaze paints and luster makes brilliant results on porcelain.

　The merit of in-glaze painting is that paints go through the glaze completely, so the surface of the porcelain is smooth even after firing just like unpainted porcelain area. Therefore, we can apply regular paints or luster just like painting on unpainted porcelain surface. Lusters do not ruin their brilliance on the in-glaze colors so the blue luster becomes deeper blue when combined with blue in-glaze color.

　Blue in-glaze colors make fine colors together with mother-of-pear luster or blue luster. The combinations are shown on my pieces in some forms.

　The firing temperature of in-glaze painting is so high that we have to finish this step before firing regular paints, which is at lower temperature.

[例] 深海に牡丹 (18頁)
Peonies on the Deep Ocean (p. 18)

[例] 菊の丸窓 (10頁)
Round Windows of Chrysanthemums (p. 10)

[例] 伊万里風牡丹皿 (6頁)
Grand Imari (p. 6)

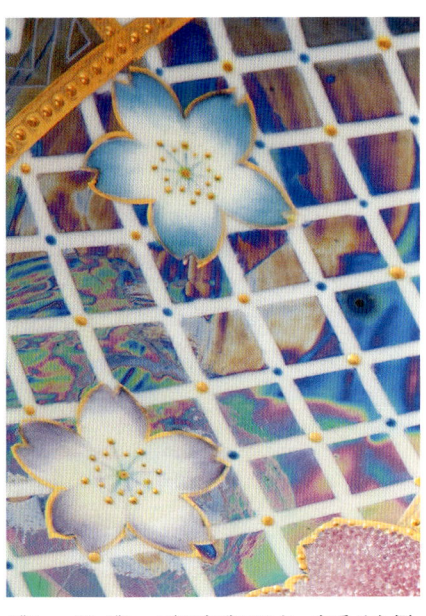

ブルーイングレーズに水色ラスターを乗せた例
The example of blue luster on blue in-glaze paint.

ブルーイングレーズに真珠ラスターを乗せた例
The example of mother-of-pearl luster on blue in-glaze paint.

ブルーイングレーズに真珠ラスターを乗せた例
The example of mother-of-pearl luster on blue in-glaze paint.

6 鯉は白い部分から描き始める。グレーで影を付け、白は白磁の色で表現する。
Start painting from the white body shading with Gray.

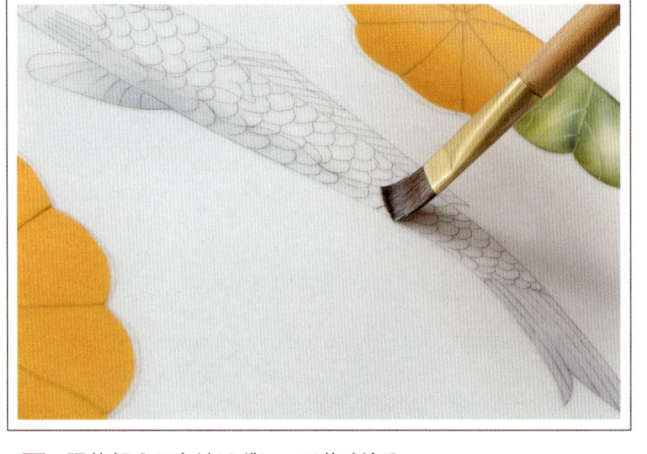

7 胴体部分の白地はグレーで薄く塗る。
Paint the white area all over with Pale Gray.

8 鰭と鼻先にイエローを入れる。髭は丸筆を使ってグレーで描く。
Add Yellow on the top of the fins and nose. Paint whiskers Gray with a liner brush.

9 赤い部分をアイアンレッドで塗る。黒の部分はブラックとロイヤルバイオレットの混色（1:1）で塗る。
Paint red area with Iron Red. Paint black area with the mixed color of Black and Royal Violet (1:1).

10 鰭の線をゴムピックで抜く。
Wipe out the line on the fin with a wipe out tool.

11 うろこ模様をゴムピックで抜く。
Wipe out the scale line with a wipe out tool.

● イングレーズとラスター

　焼成後のイングレーズにラスターを組み合わせ、磁器の輝きをさらに際立たせるテクニックがあります。

　イングレーズで描いた作品の特徴は絵の具が完全に釉薬の中に浸み込んでいるので表面は白磁のようにつるつるに仕上がることです。ですからその上に、白磁に描くように上絵の具を重ねることもできますし、ラスターも光沢を失わずにきれいに乗せることができます。上に乗せたラスターの色と土台のイングレーズの色が融合し、深い味わいのある色になります。

　たとえばブルーイングレーズの上に水色ラスターを乗せることでイングレーズ絵の具またはラスター単独では表現しきれない深いブルーを表現することができます。ブルーイングレーズと真珠ラスター、ブルーイングレーズと水色ラスターは特に相性の良い組み合わせとして私の作品でもさまざまな形で応用しています。

　イングレーズの焼成は大変高温なので、上絵付けとの組み合わせをする場合、必ず最初に焼成を行います。

In-glaze painting with luster

The combination of in-glaze paints and luster makes brilliant results on porcelain.

The merit of in-glaze painting is that paints go through the glaze completely, so the surface of the porcelain is smooth even after firing just like unpainted porcelain area. Therefore, we can apply regular paints or luster just like painting on unpainted porcelain surface. Lusters do not ruin their brilliance on the in-glaze colors so the blue luster becomes deeper blue when combined with blue in-glaze color.

Blue in-glaze colors make fine colors together with mother-of-pear luster or blue luster. The combinations are shown on my pieces in some forms.

The firing temperature of in-glaze painting is so high that we have to finish this step before firing regular paints, which is at lower temperature.

[例] 深海に牡丹 (18頁)
Peonies on the Deep Ocean (p. 18)

[例] 菊の丸窓 (10頁)
Round Windows of Chrysanthemums (p. 10)

[例] 伊万里風牡丹皿 (6頁)
Grand Imari (p. 6)

ブルーイングレーズに水色ラスターを乗せた例
The example of blue luster on blue in-glaze paint.

ブルーイングレーズに真珠ラスターを乗せた例
The example of mother-of-pearl luster on blue in-glaze paint.

ブルーイングレーズに真珠ラスターを乗せた例
The example of mother-of-pearl luster on blue in-glaze paint.

和のモチーフを描く
Painting traditional Japanese patterns

鯉と蓮の葉の皿　Carp and Lotus Leaves　D 27.0 cm

［ 筆 ］平筆10号、12号、ディテールライナー
［ 絵の具 ］
蓮の葉：ブラック、ネイプルスイエロー、オリーブグリーンNo.1、
　　　　インペリアルグリーン
鯉：グレー、ネイプルスイエロー、アイアンレッド、ブラック、ロイヤルバイオレット
［ オイル ］遅乾性ペインティングオイル
［ その他の道具・材料 ］ゴムピック、メタリックゴールドの転写紙
［ 焼成温度 ］780℃

36頁の作品のデザインを簡略化して丸皿に応用しました。
鯉の簡単な描き方と、転写紙を使った1回焼成のテクニックを説明します。

※107頁に下絵を掲載。
The line drawing is on p. 107.

Brushes: flat square brush No.10, No.12, liner brush
Paints: Lotus leaves: Black, Mixing Yellow, Olive Green, Imperial Green
Carp: Gray, Mixing Yellow, Iron Red, Black, Royal Violet
Oil: painting oil
Materials and tools: wipeout tooll, decal of metallic gold
Temperature: 780℃ (cone 016).

This is a simplified design of the piece on p.36.
　An easy one fire technique painting of carp and lotus leaves using decal are explained below.

1 メタリックゴールドの無地転写紙を用意し、蓮の葉をトレースしハサミで切り抜く。
Trace the pattern of lotus leaves on the decal and cut out with scissors.

2 転写紙を水に浸し、台紙を剥がす。
Dip the decal and remove the base coat of the decal.

3 転写紙を磁器に貼り付け、ティッシュペーパーなどで軽く押さえて空気を抜く。
Put the decal on the plate and wipe it with tissue paper to exclude the air under the decal.

4 2枚の転写紙を貼ったところ。
Two decal pieces are set on the plate.

5 緑色の蓮の葉と鯉をトレースし、葉を描く。
Trace the line drawing of carp and lotus leaves beside the decals. Paint leaves.

61

6 鯉は白い部分から描き始める。グレーで影を付け、白は白磁の色で表現する。
Start painting from the white body shading with Gray.

7 胴体部分の白地はグレーで薄く塗る。
Paint the white area all over with Pale Gray.

8 鰭と鼻先にイエローを入れる。髭は丸筆を使ってグレーで描く。
Add Yellow on the top of the fins and nose. Paint whiskers Gray with a liner brush.

9 赤い部分をアイアンレッドで塗る。黒の部分はブラックとロイヤルバイオレットの混色（1：1）で塗る。
Paint red area with Iron Red. Paint black area with the mixed color of Black and Royal Violet (1:1).

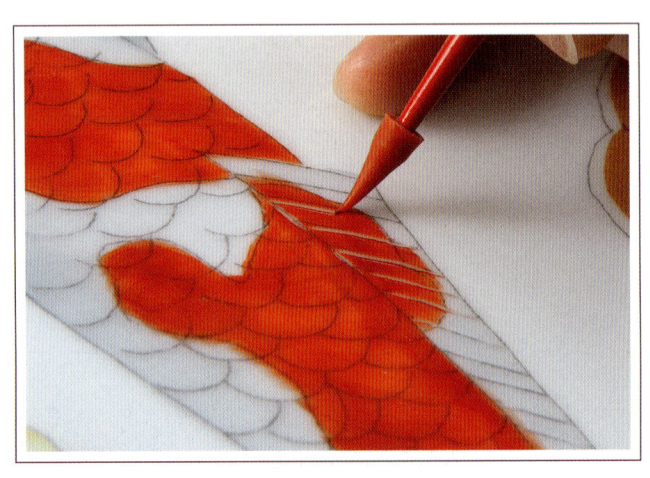

10 鰭の線をゴムピックで抜く。
Wipe out the line on the fin with a wipe out tool.

11 うろこ模様をゴムピックで抜く。
Wipe out the scale line with a wipe out tool.

12 目を描く。黒目はドーナツ状に描いて中を塗り、ハイライトを残す。
Paint eyes with black. The pupil should be painted like a doughnut.

13 鯉を描き終えたところ。この後、同様にもう1匹の鯉を描く。
The painting result of carp. Paint another carp as the same way.

14 ブラックを調合油で溶き、転写紙の葉の上に影を描く。
Shade the decal with Black.

15 葉脈をゴムピックで抜く。
Wipe out the veins with a wipe out tool.

16 780℃で焼成して完成。
Fire at 780℃ (cone 016).

63

霜降り模様の鶴の皿　A Crane with Frosty Texture　D 27.0 cm

［筆］平筆6号、8号、10号、丸筆2号、ディテールライナー
［絵の具］
鶴：ブラック、ロイヤルバイオレット、グレー、バイオレットオブアイアン、ネイプルスイエロー
牡丹：ネイプルスイエロー、オリーブグリーンNo.1、ブラックグリーンNo.2、パープルピンク、ローズマロン、グレー、インペリアルグリーン
縁飾り：ブラック、メタリックゴールド、バイオレットオブアイアン
［オイル］遅乾性ペインティングオイル
［その他の道具・材料］ゴムピック、マスキングテープ、食品用ラップ
［焼成温度］780℃

　ここでは先に、牡丹と黒い縁の下地(ブラックでパディング)と赤い線(バイオレットオブアイアン)を描いて焼成した後からの描き方を説明します。ここで焼成せずに全体を1回焼成で仕上げることもできますが、その場合には、黒縁と赤線は絵の具を水溶性のスクラッチリキッドで溶きパディングして乾燥させます。

※108頁に下絵を掲載。
The line drawing is on the p. 108.

Brushes: flat square bush No.6, No.8, No.10, round brush No.2, liner brush
Paints: Crane: Black, Royal Violet, Gray, Violet of Iron, Mixing Yellow
Peony: Mixing Yellow, Olive Green No.1, Black Green No.2, Purple Pink, Rose Maroon, Gray, Darkest Green
Texture: Black, metallic gold, Violet of Iron
Oil: painting oil
Materials and tools: wipeout tool, masking tape, cling film
Temperature: 780℃ (cone 016).

The painting of a crane, a traditional Japanese pattern symbolizing happiness, is shown on this page.
　In this page, we start painting from a crane, the texture and then the peonies were fired. We can paint all the design with one firing if we use water-based medium.

1. 牡丹と縁の黒地と赤い線を先に描き焼成しておく。鶴をトレースする。
Black, red line and peonies are fired. Trace the line drawing of the crane.

2. トレースした鶴を外側の羽から描き始める。ここではブラックとロイヤルバイオレットの混色 (1:1) を使う。
After tracing, start from the black feathers, mixing Black and Royal Violet (1:1).

3. 羽の中心をゴムピックで抜く。
Wipe out the veins with a wipe out tool.

4. 首の部分も同じ色で描き、ゴムピックで抜いて毛の質感を表現する。
Paint the neck with the same color and wipe out the hair line.

5. 白い羽は白磁の色を生かすため毛の硬い丸筆で羽の先端をしっかりと抜く。
Wipe out the white feathers with synthetic round brush.

6. 羽の内側にグレーで影を入れる。
Shade the white feathers with Gray.

7 羽の中心をゴムピックで抜く。
Wipe out the veins with a wipe out tool.

8 長い羽も同様に描く。
Paint the long feathers as the same way.

9 平筆で胸に影を入れて丸みのある立体感を表現する。
Shade the body with Gray to make it three dimensional.

10 くちばしをイエローで描く。
Paint the beak with Mixing Yellow.

11 ブラックで目を描く。ドーナツの輪のように黒目を描いて中を塗り、ハイライトを残す。
Paint eyes with Black. The pupil should be painted like a doughnut to produce the high lights.

12 くちばしに濃いイエローを重ね、頭頂の赤い部分を描く。
Add Mixing Yellow on the beak and paint head with Violet of Iron.

66

13 ブラックとグレーの混色（1：1）で足を描き、ゴムピックで節を抜く。
Paint legs with the mixing color of Black and Gray (1:1) and wipe out the joints with a wipe out tool.

14 780℃で焼成。
Fire at 780℃ (cone 016).

15 中央の四角い部分の内側をマスキングテープで、その外の牡丹を赤のマスキング液でマスキングする。
Put masking tape inside of the black area. Apply red resist on the peonies.

16 ラップを細かくたたむ。
Fold the cling film randomly.

17 メタリックゴールドをペインティングオイルで中濃ソース程度に溶き、ラップで黒地にパディングする。
Mix Metallic Gold with painting oil like sauce and pad it with folded cling film on the black area.

18 パディングを終えてマスキングを剥がしたところ。この後780℃で焼成する。
Remove the masking tape. Fire at 780℃ (cone 016).

67

牡丹の丸皿　A Peony with Black Rope　D 27.0 cm

[筆] 平筆6号、8号、10号、丸筆2号、ディテールライナー、エナメル用の筆
[絵の具] パープルピンク、ローズピンク、ローズマロン、ライラック、ロイヤルバイオレット
[オイル] 遅乾性ペインティングオイル
[その他の道具・材料] 赤のマスキング液、ゴムピック
[焼成温度] 780℃

　花弁が複雑に入り組んだ牡丹の花を1回焼成で描きます。この方法は牡丹に限らず藤などの描き方に応用することもできます。
　ここでは、牡丹の花を描く方法のみ説明します。

※109頁に下絵を掲載。
The line drawing is on p. 109.

Brushes: flat square bush No.6, No.8, No.10, round brush No.2, liner brush, mini liner
Paints: Peony: Purple Pink, Rose Pink, Rose Maroon, Lilac, Royal Violet
Leaves: Mixing Yellow, Chrome Green, Darkest Green
Rope: Black, metallic gold
Oil: painting oil
Materials and tools: red resist, wipeout tool
Temperature: 780℃ (cone 016).

Painting a peony can be done with one firing. This technique can also be applied for painting wisteria.

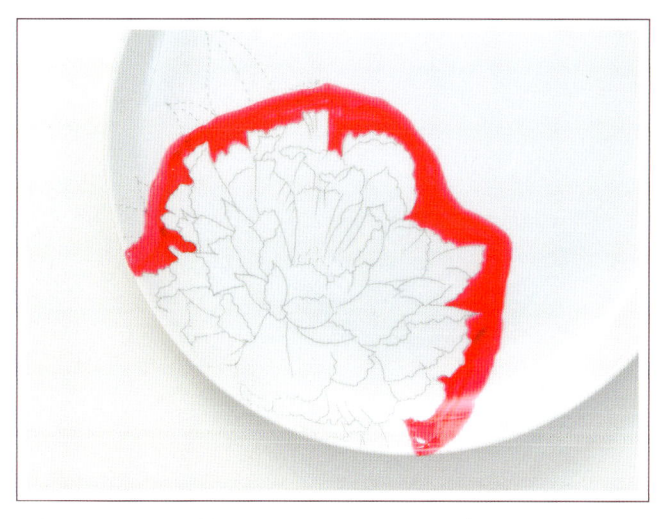

1 トレースした牡丹の周囲を赤のマスキング液で塗り乾かす。
Apply red resist outside of the tracing pattern.

2 淡い色から順番に花全体を平筆で塗る。花弁ごとに色の区別はしない。
Start painting from pale colors color on all over the flower.

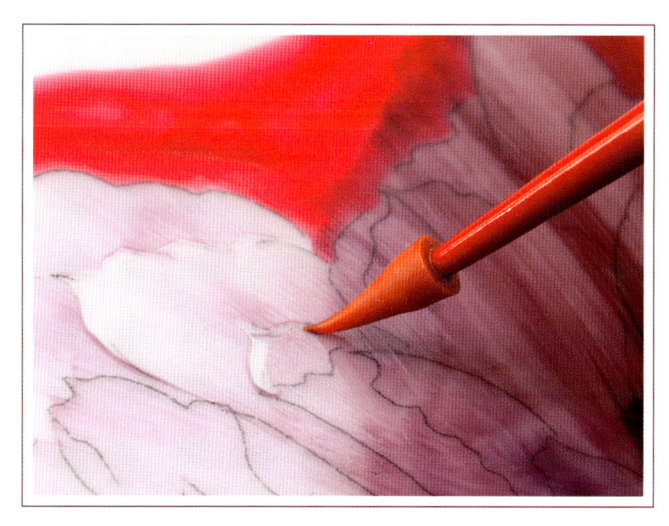

3 外側の花びらから順にゴムピックを使い花弁の縁を抜く。
Wipe out the top of the outline of the petals with a wipe out tool.

4 抜いた部分から、平筆で引っ張るように色を抜きながら描いていく。
Pull the paints away from the line with the brush.

5 濃い部分も同様に抜く。
Wipeout all the petals as the same way.

6 平筆を引いて先端の色を中心に向かって寄せるようにぼかしていく。
Pull the brush toward the center of the flower.

69

7 最後に中心のカップの部分を描く。
Wipe out the cup of the flower at the last step.

8 花芯をゴムピックで抜く。
Wipe out the pollen with a wipeout tool.

9 イエローエナメル（エナメルフリットとイエロー7：3）で花芯を盛る。
Apply Yellow enamel (enamel frit and yellow 7:3) on the pollen.

10 マスキングを剥がす。
Remove the masking.

11 牡丹を描き終えたところ。
Before firing.

12 780℃で焼成後。
After firing at 780℃ (cone 016).

● **伝統の文様を描く**

　日本には古くは着物の柄として使われた数多くの伝統的な文様がありますが、その中で磁器絵付けにも応用しやすい3つの文様の描き方を説明します。一度文様の構成を覚えれば、大きさの異なる文様を自分で作ったり、トレースが難しい立体面にフリーハンドで描いたりすることもできます。

Drawing traditional Japanese patterns
In Japan we have lots of traditional popular patterns originating from kimono design applied on the porcelain. These three patterns are the most popular for porcelains. Once you understand the drawing manner, you could draw them freehand on every piece of any size.

◇ 麻の葉文様　Pattern of hemp leaves

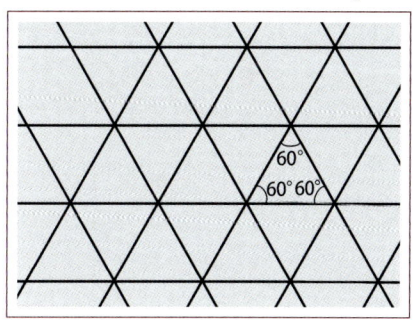

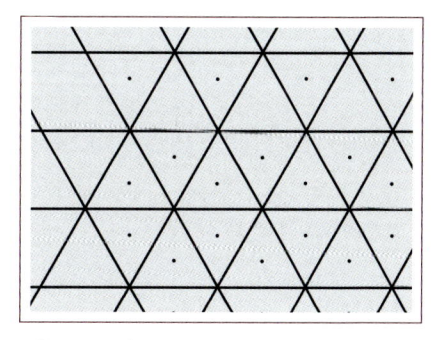

1 等間隔の平行線を引いた後、最初の線に60°で交わる2本の線を加え、たくさんの正三角形を描く。
Draw paralleled lines in a equal space. Then draw zig-zag lines across to connect the peak points of each triangle.

2 正三角形の中心部分に点を打つ。
Put dots on the center of each triangle.

3 点から3隅に向かって直線を引く。その集合体が麻の葉文様になる。
Connect the lines from the dot to the 3 corners of the triangle, and so on to form hemp leaves.

◇ 青海波（ヨーロッパでは鱗模様と呼ばれています）　Pattern of waves (It is called scales in some countries.)

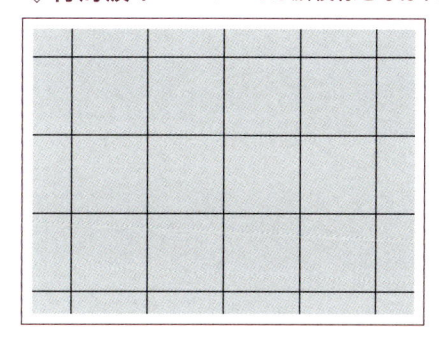

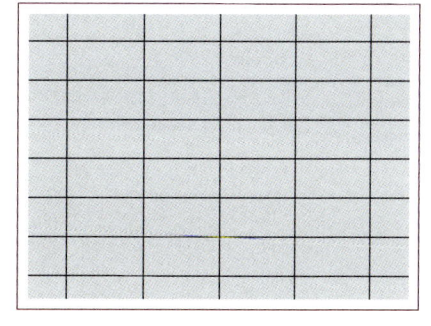

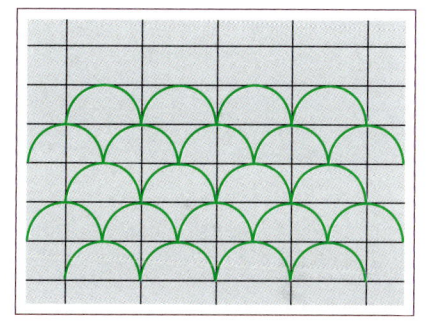

1 直角に交わる線を交差させ、たくさんの正方形を作る。
Drawing vertical lines crossing horizontal lines in equal distances produces squares.

2 正方形を等分する直線を引いて半分の大きさの長方形を作る。
By drawing horizontal lines across from left to right in the middle of each square, rectangles are produced.

3 下の長方形から波を描く。その上の波は下の波の頂点から描き始める。
Draw an arc from the bottom left corner to the right corner making sure the middle of the arc is touching the dividing line. Repeat the sequence going up.

◇ 花文様　Flower Pattern

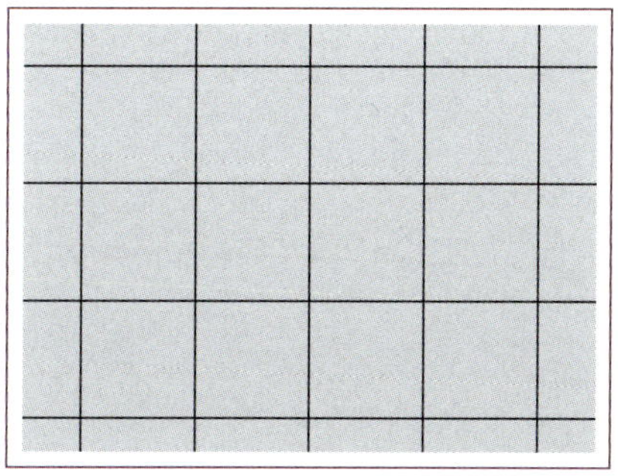

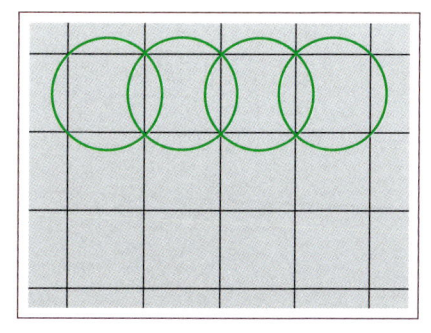

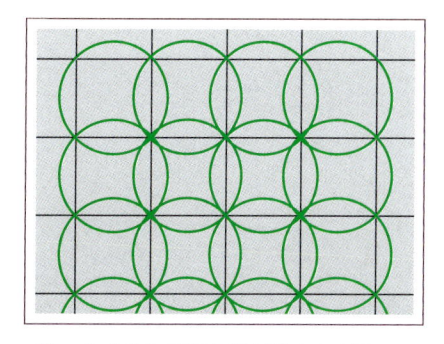

1 直角に交わる線を交差させてたくさんの正方形を作る。
Drawing vertical lines crossing horizontal lines in equal distances produces squares.

2 正方形の外側に、4隅に接触するように正円形を描き重ねる。
Start from top. Draw a circle passing through the intersections of the 4 corners of the squares. Work from left to right repeating the sequence.

3 たくさんの花文様が出来上がる。
Continue the same sequence going down, working from left to right. The resulting design of flowers is attained.

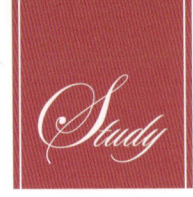

Study 1
スタディー1
宇宙のクリスマス（19頁）

制作のポイント

- 焼成前のラスターに、水溶性のメディウムで溶いた絵の具やエナメルを乗せて描く。
- ラスターの墨はじき。
- 焼成したラスターに別の色のラスターを乗せて、色の変化を楽しむ。
- 透明盛りを使い丸いエナメルボールを作る。

[筆] 平筆2号、8〜12号、ディテールライナー、盛り用ライナー筆、ラスター用平筆

[絵の具] オリーブグリーンNo.I、グレー、ネイプルスイエロー、アップルグリーン、アイビーグリーン、バイオレットオブアイアン、レッドブラウン、ピーコックブルー、シルバースノウ（メタリックホワイト）、メタリックゴールド、ホワイト、真珠ラスター、水色ラスター

[オイル] 遅乾性ペインティングオイル、エナメルオイル、スクラッチリキッド、ラスター油

[その他の道具・材料] ガラスビーズL、エナメルフリット、赤のマスキング液、墨汁、ペン、スクラッチスティック、ゴムピック、スポンジ

[焼成温度] 780℃

■ 第1焼成まで

1：ポインセチアとヒイラギの葉、大きいリボンをトレースする。
2：ヒイラギの葉の周りとヒイラギの実を赤のマスキング液でマスキングする（5mm幅厚塗り）。
3：アイビーグリーンをスクラッチリキッドでゆるめに溶き、平筆で緑のヒイラギの葉を塗る。
4：メタリックゴールドをスクラッチリキッドでゆるめに溶き、平筆で金色のヒイラギの葉を塗りスポンジで軽くたたく。絵の具を完全に乾燥させてマスキングを剥がす。
5：ポインセチアが白地と接触する部分の内側を3mm幅で赤のマスキング液を使ってマスキングする。
6：オリーブグリーンとグレーを1：1で混色しペインティングオイルで溶いて、ポインセチアの影を平筆で描く。
7：ポインセチアの葉脈をディテールライナーで抜く。
8：ヒイラギとポインセチアの周囲の皿全体に真珠ラスターを絵の具に重ならないように注意深く塗り、赤のマスキング液を剥がす。
9：エナメルフリットとメタリックゴールドを1：1の割合でスクラッチリキッドでゆるめに溶き、水溶性のゴールドエナメルを作る。
10：ゴールドエナメルでリボンの輪郭と内側の丸い模様を盛り用の筆を使って描く。780℃で焼成。

■ 第2焼成まで

11：皿をテレピンで拭く。これはラスターや金の上に赤のマスキング液を塗って剥がす時には忘れてはならない作業。忘れて直接マスキング液を塗った場合には剥がれなくなり、結局やり直すことになる。
12：ロープをトレースする。他の模様はトレースせずに後で直接描く。

{ Study 1 }
Cosmic Christmas (p. 19)

Points to learn on this subject:
- Water-based paints and enamel can be applied on the unfired luster.
- Indian ink for Japanese calligraphy can be used as a luster resist.
- Some luster can produce interesting color when applied over luster of a different color.
- Solid round ball can be made with enamel frit.

Brush: flat brush No2 and No.8 to 12, liner brush, scroller, brush for luster
Paints: Olive Green, Gray, Mixing Yellow, Apple Green, Ivy Green, Iron Red, Red Brown, Peacock Blue, metallic white, metallic gold, White, mother-of-pearl luster, blue luster
Oil: painting oil, enamel oil, scratch liquid
Materials and tools: glass beads L, enamel frit, red resist, Indian ink, pen, scratch stick, wipe out tool, sponge
Temperature: 780℃ (cone 016)

First firing

1. Trace poinsettia, holly and ribbon.
2. Apply red resist outside of the holly leaves and on the holly berries. Apply resist thickly to prevent the contamination with the water-based medium.
3. Mix Ivy Green with watery-scratch liquid and paint it on green holly leaves with a flat brush.
4. Mix Metallic Gold with watery-scratch liquid and pad the metallic mixture with a sponge on the gold holly leaves. Dry them and remove the red resist.
5. Resist inside the outline of poinsettia. The resist should be 3 mm width.
6. Mix Olive Green and Gray 1:1 with painting oil. Paint the shadow of the petals of poinsettia.
7. Wipe out the veins with liner brush.
8. Apply mother-of-pearl luster on the plate carefully avoiding the unfired paints. Remove the red resist.
9. Mix enamel frit and Metallic Gold 1:1 with watery-scratch liquid to make water-based enamel.
10. Apply Gold enamel to illustrate the texture of the ribbon. Fire at 780℃ (cone 016).

Second firing

11. Wipe the plate with turpentine. This step is important to prevent red resist sticked too much on the luster. The turpentine-wipe will facilitate the removal of red resist after it is dried.

プロセス1〜10

プロセス11〜17

プロセス18〜26

13：金のヒイラギの周囲を赤のマスキング液でマスキングする。
14：レッドブラウンをスクラッチリキッドでゆるめに溶いて平筆で金のヒイラギに影を描き葉脈をゴムピックで抜く。乾燥後マスキングを剥がす。
15：ロープを赤のマスキング液でマスキングする。
16：メタリックホワイトをスクラッチリキッドでゆるめに溶き、ポインセチアを筆で塗り軽くパディングする。
17：墨汁をペンに付けて背景の模様を描く。一部は筆で塗りつぶしスクラッチスティックで模様を抜く。雪の結晶と花模様の中心（白盛りする部分）は抜いておく。
18：ポインセチアとヒイラギ、リボン以外の皿全体に水色ラスターを塗り乾かす。
19：アップルグリーンとエナメルフリットを3：7の割合でエナメルオイルで硬く溶きボールを作る。
20：イエローとエナメルフリットを3：7の割合でエナメルオイルで硬く溶き小さめのボールを作る。

12. Trace the rope. The other patterns should be drawn freehand.
13. Apply red resist outside of the gold holly leaves.
14. Mix Red Brown with watery-scratch liquid and paint the shadow on the gold leaves. Wipe out the veins with a wipe out tool. Dry the resist completely and remove it.
15. Apply red resist on the rope.
16. Mix Metallic White with watery-scratch liquid and paint it on the whole area of the poinsettia and then pad on it with a sponge.
17. Pen the patterns of the background with Indian ink. Paint some of the leaves with a brush and scratch the pattern on them just after the ink dried. Wipe out the center of the flowers and the snow forms.
18. Apply blue luster on the background.
19. Make solid enamel ball by mixing enamel frit and Apple Green 7:3 and blend together with enamel oil.
20. Make smaller solid enamel balls by mixing enamel frit and Mixing Yellow 7:3 and blend together with enamel oil.
21. Put yellow enamel ball on top of the green enamel ball to make two color balls like eyeballs. Put them on the center of the poinsettia.
22. Mix enamel frit and White 1:1 with watery-scratch liquid. Paint stars and apply dots on the unfired luster.

73

21：緑のボールに黄色のボールを重ね、目玉のような一つのボールにまとめる。それをポインセチアの中心に付ける。
22：エナメルフリットとホワイトを1:1の割合でスクラッチリキッドでゆるめに溶き、星やドットを盛る。
23：バイオレットオブアイアンをペインティングオイルで溶きヒイラギの実を描く。
24：エナメルフリットとピーコックブルーを7:3の割合でスクラッチリキッドでゆるめに溶き、リボンの穴の所々に盛る。
25：エナメルフリットとメタリックホワイトをスクラッチリキッドでゆるめに溶き、皿の縁にスポンジでたたいて雪のような装飾を作る。
26：Lサイズのガラスビーズに糊（エナメルフリットをスクラッチリキッドで溶く）を付け、皿の全体に散りばめるように貼り付ける。780℃で焼成。

23. Mix Iron Red with painting oil and paint the holly berries.
24. Mix enamel frit and Peacock Blue with watery-scratch liquid to make blue enamel. Apply the blue enamel on the holes of the ribbon randomly.
25. Mix enamel frit and Metallic White with watery-scratch liquid and apply it like snow on the edge of the plate with a sponge.
26. Make glue by mixing enamel frit with scratch liquid. Put glass beads L with the glue on the plate randomly. Fire at 780 ℃(cone 016).

◇2色のエナメルボールの作り方

前著ではホワイトエナメルを使って白いボールを作る方法をご紹介しましたが、エナメルフリットを使うと、絵の具の色を生かしたボールを作ることができます。ここでは、「宇宙のクリスマス」でアクセント的に使っている2色のボールを作る方法を説明します。

How to make a double color ball

Although the way to make ball with white enamel was shown on my former book, we can make a double-color ball with enamel frit. This is the explanation how to make it on the study of "Cosmic Christmas."

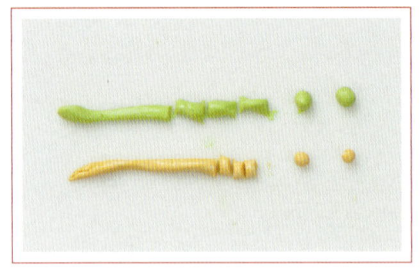

1 エナメルフリットとアップルグリーン、エナメルフリットとネイブルスイエローを、それぞれエナメルオイルで粘土状に練り、緑と黄色のボールを作る。黄色は緑の半分程度の大きさにする。
Prepare 2 colors of clay ball : for green ball, mix enamel frit and Apple Green with enamel oil and for yellow ball, mix enamel frit and Mixing Yellow with enamel oil. Yellow ball should be half in size of a green ball.

2 緑のボールの中央にゴムピックで窪みを作る。
Make a well on the center of green ball with a wipeout tool.

3 2色のボールを重ね、軽く丸める。
Set the yellow ball on the well of the green ball and roll them together.

4 軽く押して磁器に定着させる。780℃で焼成する。
Apply and fire at 780℃ (cone 016).

同じ方法でロイヤルバイオレットとピーコックブルーの2色のボールを作り、トンボの目玉を表現しました。
The eyeballs of the dragonfly can be made by the same way with royal violet and Peacock Blue. Put masking tape on the inner side of the rim.

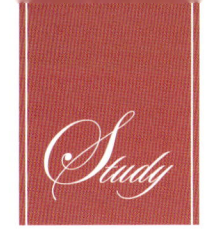

Study 2
スタディー2
暁の蓮（20頁）

制作のポイント
- ガラスビーズで装飾する。
- 金の上にラップを使ったテクスチャーを作る。
- 水溶性メディウムを使って色盛り（エナメリング）する。

[筆] 平筆8～16号、ディテールライナー、盛り用ライナー筆、ワイプアウト用丸筆、金用筆、ラスター用平筆

[絵の具] 葉：ネイプルスイエロー、オリーブグリーンNo.1、インペリアルグリーン
　蓮の花：パープルピンク、ローズピンク、ライラック、グレー、オリーブグリーンNo.1
　その他：ホワイト、ブラック、ロイヤルバイオレット、ピーコックブルー、メタリックホワイト、メタリックゴールド、真珠ラスター、水色ラスター、19％マット金

[オイル] 遅乾性ペインティングオイル、スクラッチリキッド、エナメルオイル（バルサム、ミネラルオイル1：1）、金油、ラスター油、テレピン

[その他の道具・材料] 赤のマスキング液、エナメルフリット、ガラスビーズM、食品用ラップ、スクラッチスティック、スポンジ、ドライヤー

[焼成温度] 780℃、760℃、720℃

■ 第1焼成まで
1：デザインをトレースし、蓮の葉の周りに赤のマスキング液を塗り乾燥させる。
2：16号の筆でネイプルスイエロー、オリーブグリーンNo.1、インペリアルグリーンの順に、蓮の葉を中心に向かい葉脈に沿って塗り、マスキングを剥がす。
3：茎と、下の方の蓮の花弁の内側をオリーブグリーンNo.1で塗る。

プロセス1～6

プロセス7～10

{ Study 2 }
Heavenly Lotus (p. 20)

Points to learn on this subject:
- Glass-beading.
- Creating texture with cling film on gold.
- Enameling with water-based medium.

Brushes: flat brushes No.8 to 16, liner brush, scroller, synthetic round brush No.2, brushes for gold and luster

Paints: Leaves: Mixing Yellow, Olive Green No.1, Darkest Green
Lotus: Purple Pink, Rose Pink, Lilac No.2, Gray, Olive Green No.1
Other colors: White, Black, Mixing Yellow, Royal Violet, Peacock Blue, metallic white, metallic gold, 19% liquid gold
Luster: mother-of-pearl luster, blue luster
Oil: Painting oil, scratch liquid, enamel oil (balsam of copaiba and mineral oil 1:1), gold thinner, luster thinner, turpentine
Materials and tools: red resist, enamel frit, Glass Beads M, cling film, scratch stick, sponge, handy dryer
Temperature: 780℃ (cone 016), 760℃ (cone 017), 720℃ (cone 018)

First firing
1. Trace the design. Resist outside of the leaves.
2. Paint leaves with Mixing Yellow, Olive Green No.1 and Darkest Green. Remove the resist.
3. Paint stems and shadow area of the lower lotus with Olive Green No.1.
4. Paint pink lotus with Purple Pink, Lilac No.2 and Rose Pink.
5. Paint white lotus with Gray and Lilac No.2.

プロセス11〜19　　　　　　　　　　　　プロセス20〜31

4：ピンクの蓮の花をパープルピンク、ライラックNo.2、ローズピンクで描く。
5：白い蓮の花をグレー、ライラックNo.2で描く。
6：イエローエナメル（エナメルフリット、イエロー7：3）でピンクの蓮の花弁を縁取る。780℃で焼成。

■ 第2焼成まで
7：真珠ラスターと水色ラスターを塗るために、焼成後の絵の縁に赤のマスキング液を塗る。
8：背景に真珠ラスターを塗る。
9：蓮の葉の翻った部分に水色ラスターを塗る。
10：ラスターに絵の具が触れないように気を付けて花や葉に色を足す。780℃で焼成。

■ 第3焼成まで
11：テレピンで皿を拭き、鉛筆で皿の縁に入れた金の線の下描きをする。
12：背景のメタリック絵の具の葉と水色ラスターの周囲に赤のマスキング液を塗る。
13：メタリックホワイトをスクラッチリキッドでゆるめに溶いて右背景の葉と水色ラスターの上をスポンジで塗る。
14：メタリックゴールドをスクラッチリキッドでゆるめに溶いて左背景の葉を塗る。乾燥させて赤のマスキングを取り除く。
15：乾燥したメタリック絵の具の葉にスクラッチスティックで模様を描く。絵の具の粉は乾いた筆で取り除く。
16：赤のマスキング液で右下の金の葉の周りをマスキングして乾かす。
17：19％マット金を筆で塗りスポンジで軽くパディングする。マスキングを取り除く。
18：皿の縁に金の線を描く。
19：ピンクの蓮の縁取りの上に金を塗る。760℃で焼成。

■ 第4焼成まで
20：テレピンで皿を拭き、右下の金の葉の周りに赤のマスキング液を塗り乾燥させる。
21：エナメルフリットをエナメルオイルで溶き、ガラス用の糊を作る。ガラスビーズを付けたい花弁に糊を塗る。

6. Prepare yellow enamel by mixing enamel frit and Mixing Yellow 7:3, blend together with enamel oil and apply on the petal edge of the pink lotus. Fire at 780℃ (cone 016).

Second firing
7. Resist lotus flower and around painted area and gold space adjacent to luster.
8. Apply mother-of-pearl luster on the background.
9. Apply blue luster on the flip side of the lower leaf, let dry and remove resist.
10. Strengthen paints on the painted area carefully not to touch unfired luster. Fire at 780℃ (cone 016).

Third firing
11. Clean the plate with turpentine. Draw border line with a pencil.
12. Resist 3 areas for metallic painting: (1) upper right side, (2) left side, (3) flip side of leaf. Do only around assigned area.
13. Mix Metallic White with watery-scratch liquid. Sponge it on the upper right area of the background and on the blue luster painted leaf.
14. Mix Metallic Gold with watery-scratch liquid. Sponge it on the left area of the background. Dry them completely and remove the red resist.
15. Scratch the pattern on the dried metallic paints with a wooden stick. Remove the dust with a dry brush.
16. Resist outer line of the gold leaf.
17. Paint mat gold and pad on it with a sponge gently. Remove the resist.
18. Draw the border line with gold.
19. Paint gold on the yellow enamel on the petals of the pink lotus. Fire at 760℃ (cone 017).

Fourth firing
20. Clean the plate with turpentine. Apply red resist outside of the gold area.

22：Mサイズのガラスビーズを糊の上にたっぷりとかける。皿を裏返して余分なビーズを落とす。
23：ブラックをペインティングオイルで溶き金の上に塗る。ラップをくしゃくしゃにしてその上に置き、しっかりと押さえて剥がす。葉脈をゴムピックで抜く。
24：葉の明るい部分に露を描く。
25：エナメルオイルでホワイトエナメル（エナメルフリットとホワイト1:1）を作る。同様の方法でブラックエナメル（エナメルフリット、ブラック1:1）とメタリックゴールドエナメル（エナメルフリット、メタリックゴールド1:1）も作る。
26：ブラックエナメルで右下の金の葉の縁にドットを付ける。
27：ホワイトエナメルで背景と下の葉のメタリックホワイトの部分にドットを付ける。
28：メタリックゴールドエナメルで左上のメタリックゴールドの葉にドットを付ける。
29：イエローエナメルで蓮の葉に花粉を付ける。
30：エナメルフリットとホワイト（1:1）、エナメルフリットとローズピンク（7:3）でエナメルボールを作り好みの場所に付ける。
31：スクラッチリキッドを使って、ピンクエナメル（エナメルフリット、ローズピンク7:3）、バイオレットエナメル（エナメルフリット、ロイヤルバイオレット7:3）、ブルーエナメル（エナメルフリット、ピーコックブルー7:3）の3色の水溶性のエナメルを作る。これらのエナメルを、濃度を水で調整しながら筆で縁飾りの金線の枠の内側に塗る。720℃で焼成。

21. Mix enamel frit with enamel oil to make glue for glass beads. Paint the glue on your favorite petals.
22. Apply glass beads M on the petals like snow falling. Remove the extra beads by turning the plate upside down.
23. Paint Black on the gold. Place a crumpled cling film on it and push well. Remove the film. Wipe out the vein.
24. Paint dewdrops on the light area of the leaves.
25. Mix enamel frit and white 1:1 with enamel oil (balsam of copaiba and mineral oil 1:1) to make white enamel. Prepare black enamel and Metallic Gold enamel the same way.
26. Apply black enamel on the edge of the gold leave.
27. Apply white enamel on the edge and inside of white metallic decoration.
28. Apply gold enamel on the edge and inside of white metallic decoration.
29. Apply yellow enamel to indicate pollen.
30. Make solid white enamel balls by mixing enamel frit and White 1:1 with enamel oil. Make solid pink enamel balls by mixing enamel frit and Rose Pink 7:3 with enamel oil. Put them as you like.
31. Make three colors water-based enamel with scratch liquid: pink enamel (enamel frit and Rose Pink 7:3), violet enamel (enamel frit and Royal Violet 7:3) and blue enamel (enamel frit and Peacock Blue 7:3). Mix with water and paint the small squares of the hem line. Fire at 720℃ (cone 018).

◇水滴の描き方

水滴は作品にワンポイントの魅力を加えるための便利な小道具です。

この作品では、焼成後の葉の明るい部分を選んで描きました。白盛りは直径3mm以下の小さな水滴の場合は絵の具のホワイトのみを使い、大きめの水滴にはホワイトエナメル（エナメルフリット、ホワイト1:1）を使います。

[絵の具] インペリアルグリーン（または濃いグリーン）、ホワイト（またはホワイトエナメル）

How to paint the dewdrops

The dewdrops are useful item to produce charming point.

Choose the light place on the leaves to paint dewdrops. The white accent should be made with white color or the white enamel (enamel frit and white 1:1). The white color is for the size under 3 mm in diameter. The white enamel is for the size of over 3 mm.

Paints: Darkest Green, White

1 インペリアルグリーンで水滴の形を線描する。
Paint a circle with darkest green.

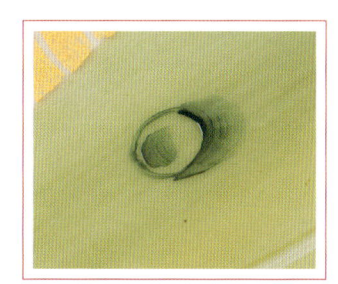

2 外側の影を描き、その反対側の内側に小さな影を入れる。
Shade the outside and inside of the circle.

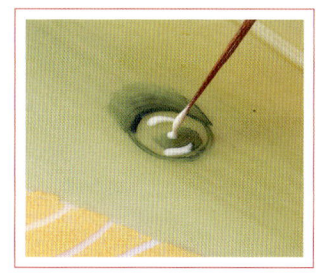

3 外の影の内側と反射光のスペースに白盛りを入れる。下と上の長さの違いは3:2ぐらい。中央にハイライトとしてドットを付ける。
Apply white scrolls and dot inside of the circle. The length of the high-light line of the upper and the lower should be 3:2.

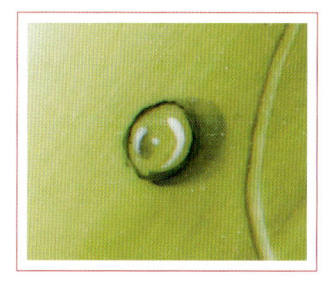

4 780℃で焼成し完成。
Fire at 780℃ (cone 016).

Study

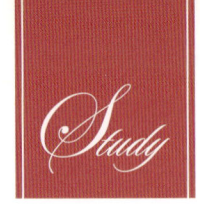

スタディー3
沖の鶴〈縁文様のみ〉(17頁)

制作のポイント
・イングレーズのペン描き。
・イングレーズのスクラッチ。
・イングレーズとラスターのコンビネーション。

[筆] 平筆No.6、No.8、ディテールライナー、盛り用ライナー筆、ラスター用平筆、金用筆

[縁飾りに使う絵の具]
真珠ラスター、ネイプルスイエロー、19%マット金
イングレーズ絵の具：染付ブルー、伊万里ブルー、ヘブンリーブルー、シンクインライラック

[中央の絵に使う絵の具（参考）]
鶴：グレー、ブラック、ロイヤルバイオレット、ネイプルスイエロー、クタニレッド
梅：グレー、ポンパドールピンク、アイアンレッド
背景と波：オーカー、イエローブラウン、ネイプルスイエロー、ピーコックブルー、ダークブルー、ホワイト

[オイル] ペンオイル、スクラッチリキッド

[その他の道具・材料] 赤のマスキング液、エナメルフリット、ペン、スクラッチスティック

[焼成温度] 780℃、1,220℃

■ 第1焼成まで
1：縁飾りの幅を決めて線を引く。
2：12分割し、境界に線を引く。
3：一マスずらして線を引き6分割する。
4：3mm幅のマスキングテープを境界線に貼り、スクラッチの部分を除き2つのパートに麻の葉模様と青海波を写し、染付ブルーでペン描きする。
5：スクラッチ部分の周囲をマスキングし、染付ブルーをスクラッチオイルで溶いてパディングし、乾燥させて唐草模様をスクラッチする。
6：ひとまず絵の具を定着させるために780℃で焼成する（仮焼成）。

■ 第2焼成まで
7：残りの3つのパートに下絵を写し、葉は伊万里ブルー、花はシンクインライラック、ヘブンリーブルー、染付ブルーで描く。1,220℃で焼成する。

■ 第3焼成まで
8：縁飾りの内側をマスキング液でマスキングし、菊の花と麻の葉模様の間と桜と青海波の間に3mmのマスキングテープを張り全体を2分割する。
9：菊の花と唐草模様、桜の側全体に真珠ラスターを塗る。
10：麻の葉模様、梅、青海波側全体にブルーマザーオブパールを塗る。
11：軽く乾かしてマスキングをはずし、780℃で焼成する。

{ Study 3 }
A Crane on the Sea - Border design (p. 17)

Points to learn on this subject:
・Penning with in-glaze paint.
・Scratching with in-glaze paint.
・Combination usage of in-glaze paint and luster.

Brushes: square brush No.6, No8, liner brush, scroller, brushes for luster and gold
Paints: MixingYellow, mother-of-pearl luster, 19% mat gold
In-glaze paints: Sometsuke-Blue, Imari-Blue, Heavenly-Blue, Sink in Lilac,
*For your reference - The paints for the picture of the center area:
Crane: Gray, Black, Royal Violet, Mixing Yellow, Kutani Red
Japanese apricot: Gray, Pompadour Pink, Iron Red
The background and waves: Ocher, Yellow Brown, Mixing Yellow, Peacock Blue, Dark Blue, White
Oil: pen oil, scratch liquid
Materials and tools: red resist, enamel frit, pen, scratch stick
Temperature: 780℃ (cone 016), 1,220℃ (cone 7)

First firing
1. Measure the width of the border and draw the line with pencil.
2. Divide the plate into 12 sections and draw the dividing line.
3. Draw the slanting lines every two sections and this makes total of 6 sections on the border.
4. Put the 3mm masking tape on the dividing line of six sections. Trace patterns of hemp leaves and waves. Pen the patterns with Sometsuke-Blue.
5. Put masking tape around the section of arabesque pattern. Mix Sometsuke-Blue with scratching liquid and pad on the area. Dry it and scratch the arabesque pattern.
6. Fire at 780℃ (cone 016) just to set the paint.

Second firing
7. Trace the three flower pattern on the remaining sections. Paint leaves with Imari-Blue. Paint flower with sink-in-Lilac, Heavenly-Blue and Sometsuke-Blue. Fire at 1,220℃ (cone 7).

Third firing
8. Apply red resist on the edge of the center area. Put 3 mm masking tape on the dividing lines between the chrysanthemum pattern and the pattern of hemp leaves, and also on the dividing line between the cherry pattern and the pattern of the waves. The border is now divided into two areas by masking tapes.

■ 第4焼成まで

12：各柄の境界線と内側の線、花芯、唐草模様、麻の葉模様、青海波の中央をイエローエナメルで盛る。780℃で焼成。

■ 第5焼成まで

13：盛りを19%マット金で伏せる。780℃で焼成。

9. Apply Mothe-of-Pearl luster on the patterns of chrysanthemum, arabesque and cherry.
10. Apply Blue mother-of-Pearl luster on the patterns of hemp leaves, Japanese apricot and waves.
11. Dry them before removing the masking tapes. Fire at 780℃ (cone 016).

Fourth firing

12. Apply dots of yellow enamel (enamel frit and Yellow 7:3) on the border line of the each section and on the center of the flower, arabesque, hemp leaves and waves. Fire 780℃ (cone 016).

Fifth firing

13. Apply 19% mat gold on the border line and enamel dots. Fire at 780℃ (cone 016).

プロセス 1〜5

プロセス 6

プロセス 7

プロセス 8〜13

79

私が使う基本の道具
Basic tools and materials

私が絵付けをするときに使っている基本的な道具類について、ご説明します。

●絵の具

私は基本的に国産の絵の具を使っています。イメージ通りの色がない場合には、メーカーにお願いしてオリジナルカラーを調合してもらいます。また、アメリカやヨーロッパの絵の具を使うこともあります。

アメリカでは絵画的な絵付けが主流であるため微妙な色合いの絵の具の種類が豊富ですが、実際には外国から輸入している絵の具も多いようです。ヨーロッパの絵の具は色そのものが美しく鮮やかなものが多いのですが、鉛の含有量が多いものもありますので、食器として使う場合には注意が必要です。

粒子が粗い絵の具は事前にアルコールで空練りすると、アルコールが蒸発した後滑らかになります。

よく使う色はミネラルオイルで溶き置きしてパーツケースに保存しています。ただし、マロン、バイオレット、ブルー、ブラックグリーンなど金系や寒色系の絵の具は長く置くと伸びが悪くなると感じるので、溶き置きせず、その都度溶くようにしています。

私は絵画的な絵付けではカドミウムやセレンを成分とする絵の具は使いません。他の成分の絵の具と接触することで黒く変色するリスクがあることと、ある程度の量を塗らないと本来の鮮やかな色が出ないため微妙なグラデーション表現には不向きであると感じるのが、その理由です。あえて使うとしたら、鮮やかな発色を生かしてポップでモダンな柄の装飾品などに使うのがよいのではないかと思います。

黒は大変はがれやすい色です。パディングやベタ塗りをするときには紫系の色を20〜50％程度混ぜて使うと、はがれを防ぐことができます。漆黒を表現したい場合には、2〜3段階に分けて徐々に色を深めていくとよいでしょう。「無鉛」あるいは「Lead Free」の表示が付いた絵の具以外の絵付け用の絵の具には、鉛が含まれています。鉛には絵の具の発色を助け磁器に定着させる作用がありますが人体には有害物質です。絵の具の粉を吸い込んだり小さな子供の手に触れることのないよう、くれぐれも取り扱いに気を付けて下さい。

●オイル

私は普段は原宿陶画舎のペインティングオイルと市販のミネラルオイルを用意し、描くものによって配分を変えながら使っています。絵の具の溶き置き用にはミネラルオイルを「溶き油」として使います。

アメリカンスタイルの作品など大きなモチーフを描く場合には、日本ヴォーグ社の描き油やアメリカのアーティストが独自に調合したオイルを使うこともあります。これらのオイルはさらりとして伸びがよく、バックグラウンドなど広い面積を塗る場合には埃の侵入も防ぎ透明感のある仕上がりが期待できます。ただし多少乾きが早いので、後から修正を必要とする人には不便な面もあります。いずれのオイルもミネラルオイルとの相性はよいので、私は常に併用しています。ミネラルオイルは大変伸びがよく、少し筆に付けるだけでスムーズな筆運びを助けてくれますが、使い過ぎると適量の絵の具が乗らず、焼成中に絵の具が流れ、跡が焼き付くことがありま

My preferred painting tools and materials are as follows.

Paints

Japanese paints are my favorite. Some of my paints are order made, blended by supplier according to my request. I also like American and European paints. American paints have various color ranges, probably because American painters prefer to paint pictorial motifs. European paints are smooth and brilliant. However, care should be taken when buying paints of unknown contents as some of them may contain too much lead. It is best to use such paints only on porcelain objects other than tableware.

When nice color but sandy paints are encountered, mix it well on the glass tile with alcohol. After evaporation, the paint's texture becomes smooth.

I do not pre-mix colored paints for storage such as maroon, violet, blue, black and some cool colors, for these colored paints in a paste form ruin in a short time. I usually mix these colors just before painting to get a smooth condition.

I do not use paints made from cadmium or selenium. As you may know, these elements could be toxic in large amount and also the color darkens easily when in contact with other paints. Caution must be observed as they can be risky to health. In addition as we need large amount to get remarkable coloring effects with the paints, it is difficult to make beautiful gradations with them. If you dare to use these paints, I recommend using them in modern and pop design.

I would like to mention about black paint. Black paint is a tricky paint as it is easy to chip off after few firings. I always use black color mixed with 20 to 50% of violet color. To prevent from chipping off, violet is the best paint to stabilize black as it complements and enhances the beauty resulting to an elegant black color. When I wish to make ultimate black, I paint with such violet-black mixture step by step at least three times to deepen the color.

Oils

The painting oil of Harajuku Togasha is practically my common oil, however sometimes I also use painting oil of Nihon Vogue-sha, with a smooth quality and convenient drying nature, which is ideal for painting large area. I prefer mineral oil as mixing oil. Mineral oil aids to make smooth brush stroke, however too much of this oil dulls the paint and also in the worst condition, the oil may run during firing.

す。

　他にも制作する作品によって様々なオイルや溶剤を使っていますので、以下に私の使用方法とともにご紹介します。

◇テレピン

　松科の樹脂油。安価で扱いやすい速乾性オイルですがアレルギー症状を引き起こす場合があり、健康上の問題から世界的には使用が減る傾向にあります。ファットオイルの希釈や、速乾絵付け、オレンジオイルと混ぜて筆洗いなどに使っています。焼成後の金やラスターに赤のマスキング液を塗る際の下塗りオイルとしても使用します。

◇ファットオイル

　一般的にはテレピンを揮発させて作るどろりとした濃縮テレピンのことを意味しますが、ヨーロッパでは単に「粘度の高いミキシングオイル」という意味で使われることもあります。ですから、ヨーロッパのペインターがファットオイルというものが、全て濃縮テレピンとはかぎりません。私はレイズドペーストを練る際にテレピンと組み合わせて使っています。

◇クローブオイル

　丁子油。速乾性のオイルとしてテレピン同様の用途で使われます。酸化防止作用があるため、筆洗いや、ヨーロピアンテクニックで使われる羽管の筆先を保管する際、保存用に筆に付けるオイルとして使う場合があります。即席のペンオイルを作るときにも使います。

◇ラベンダーオイル

　粘性のオイルの希釈用にテレピン同様の用途で使います。金の乾きを穏やかにしたい場合に金油としても使います。

◇オレンジオイル

　オレンジジュースの残りかすから抽出された成分で作られているオイルです。洗浄効果とともに筆をケアする効果があります。テレピンと１：１で混ぜて油性の速乾性オイル用の筆洗いとして使っています。

◇グラウンディングオイル

　粘度の高い速乾性オイル。グラウンディング（ドライダスト、あるいは乾式色地塗り）の際の下地オイルとして使います。

◇スクラッチリキッド

　スクラッチテクニックに最適な水溶性のメディウムです。水溶性速乾オイル程乾きが早くないので、スクラッチテクニックにかかわらず、油性オイルとの組み合わせで焼成を省いて複雑な絵付け作業を一度にこなすことができます。

◇水溶性速乾メディウム

　油性のオイルが香りや揮発力が強いのに比べると、無色透明で匂いもありません。ヨーロピアンスタイルの小花を描くときや、スクラッチテクニックを用いるときのオイルとして使います。粘度が高くなった場合には水溶性の遅乾性メディウム（水溶性ソルベント）を少量混ぜて調節します。筆洗いは水で行います。油性の

Let me explain my favorite medium collections in my drawer.

Turpentine

Generally turpentine is used as a thinner for closed mixing oil, which is cheap and useful for many types of painting, but sometimes causes allergic problem to the painter. That's why some painters exclude it from their collection. I use it as a brush cleaner together with orange oil, as a thinner for fat oil, and as a cleaning oil for fired gold and luster to be covered with red resist.

Fat oil

Generally fat oil is the mixing oil made from evaporated turpentine. However, some people call fat oil, literally meaning "sticky painting oil." So, not all fat oil is made from turpentine. I use fat oil as mixing oil for raised paste powder.

Clove oil

Clove oil is used as a thinner for closed mixing oil. It is also a nice brush cleaner and used as brush care oil. I add clove oil into my mixing oil to make pen oil.

Lavender oil

This oil is used as a thinner for closed mixing oil and also it is used as a mild gold thinner.

Orange oil

This oil is made from the refuse of orange juice. It is not only a nice cleaner but also good for brush care.

　Turpentine and orange oil are mixed 1:1 to make a cleaner for brushes used with closed medium.

Grounding oil

This is sticky closed oil which is use for grounding.

Scratch liquid

Water-based medium especially it is useful for the scratch technique. However it is not only for the scratching technique but also for painting complicated work such as overlapped painting of water-based painted area with oil-based medium or vice-versa. We can skip the firing in between and save time of firing.

Water-based closed medium

This medium has no smell and no color. I use it to paint small Dresden flower and for scratch technique. Water-based open medium or just water is the thinner for this medium.

　Water is the best brush cleaner for this medium. After applying water-based paints on the porcelain surface, oil-based paints can be painted over it, so we can do complicated work by overlapping these medium.

オイルと組み合わせて複雑な作品制作にも使います。

◇キャリングオイル

　ペインティングオイルの一種です。速乾と遅乾の中間ぐらいの、いわゆる「セミオープン」タイプの伸びのよいオイルで、中～大のヨーロピアンブーケなどを描く際に重宝します。ミネラルオイルとの相性も良好です。

◇コパイババルサム（バルサム）

　樹液をベースにした粘度の高いオイルです。絵の具の定着力に優れるので、絵付けにおいては様々な用途で使われています。ほとんどの遅乾性ペインティングオイルに含まれています。

　白磁に下絵が付きにくいとき、微量のバルサムを白磁に塗り込んでオイルの被膜を作ると、鉛筆ではっきりと描くことができます。

＊和絵付け用の膠（にかわ）にもバルサム同様の作用があります。

◇ミネラルオイル

　別名流動パラフィンとも呼称されています。化粧品などの原料にも使われる精製された透明の鉱物油です。不乾性で酸化しないため、絵付けでは主に調合油のベースとして用いられます。絵の具の溶き置き用のオイル（溶き油）にもなります。ほとんどの油性遅乾性オイルと相性がよいので、制作中の筆洗いにも便利です。

◇アクアマジック

　筆洗い専用液。水性、油性を問わずあらゆる溶剤を強力に除去すると同時に保護する効果があるので、筆を使用した後この液で汚れを落とし、水ですすいで陰干ししています。

◇FX-0131（金油・ラスター油）

　主に筆洗い用の金油、ラスター油として使っています。

◇PS-Hオイル（金油）

　固まった金を溶かす強力なオイルです。金作業のときには欠かせません。

◇アルコール（エタノール）

　白磁の汚れ落としのほか、絵付け途中の筆の強力洗浄にも使います。

●筆洗い

　普段は市販のブラシクリーナーを使っていますが、アメリカンスタイルの絵付けの途中はミネラルオイルを筆洗いに使います。油性速乾オイルの筆洗いにはテレピンとオレンジオイルを半分ずつ調合したものを用います。テレピンは洗浄と揮発作用、オレンジオイルは洗浄と筆の保護作用があります。

　水溶性のメディウムを使った場合には筆は水で洗います。筆を傷めないように水を瓶の中に入れ、その中でやさしくすすぐようにします。

　絵付け作業に一区切りついたときには、筆の隅々までしっかり洗浄すると同時に保護作用もあるアクアマジックで洗い、水ですすいで陰干しし、ケースにしまいます。筆に保存用のオイルは付けません。私は様々なオイルを使うので、特定のオイルを付けて保存することで他のオイルになじまない筆になるのを避けたいからです。ただし、水溶性メディウム用の筆と金彩用の筆、ラスター用の筆は他の筆と分けています。

Carrying oil
This is one of my painting oil which is semi-open. It's good for painting Dresden bouquet and also can be mixed with mineral oil.

Balsam of copaiba
This oil is sticky mixing oil made from copaiba tree. It supports paint to cling on to the porcelain. Most painting oil contains this oil as an essence. When I find it hard to draw with a pencil on the porcelain, a drop of balsam of copaiba is spread onto the porcelain followed by polishing the surface with a paper, with this step drawing clearly with a pencil is possible.

Mineral oil
Some people call this liquid paraffin oil, which is also used as cosmetic liquid.

As mineral oil is not oxidized, not evaporated and does not dry, we can use it as a mixing oil for paints. Since mineral oil is used as a fundamental liquid for open medium, such medium can be mixed with it. Mineral oil is my mixing oil, thinner for my painting oil, and one of brush cleaner.

Aqua Magic
This is an ultimate brush cleaner. Any medium such as oily, water-based and even gold can be washed with this cleaner. After washing with regular brush cleaner, I clean the brushes with Aqua Magic and rinse them gently with water. After that, I dry them naturally in a shaded place.

FX-0131
This is used as a luster thinner. It can be used also as a mild gold thinner.

PS-H oil
This is my favorite strong gold thinner which can liquefy harden gold easily.

Alcohol
Alcohol is my porcelain cleaner and sometimes temporary brush cleaner.

Brush cleaner
Odorless brush cleaner is my basic cleaner, however during the process of American-style painting, mineral oil is my brush cleaner. For cleaning off closed oil, such as MX54, mixed-blended cleaner of turpentine and orange oil 1:1 is the best cleaner for me. Turpentine is a strong cleaner and evaporates quickly in a short time. Orange oil not only cleans the brush but also cares for brush hair. Water is the best cleaner for water-based medium, however I always wash brushes in a small jar of water gently and refrain from washing directly under the faucet.

At the end of my daily painting, I clean all the brushes with Aqua Magic and finally rinse them with water, dry them naturally before keeping in the case. Keeping my brushes in oil is not convenient for my brushes, as my brushes

絵付け用の筆は動物毛のデリケートなものが多いので、筆の手入れはとても重要です。特にホビーペインターの場合は、毎日筆を使うわけではないので、使用後の手入れが筆の保管状態に大きく影響します。乾燥し過ぎると毛が抜ける原因になりますし、汚れが付いたまま保管するとカビの原因になります。

白毛の繊細な筆を化学繊維の筆と同様に乱暴に扱って短期間でだめにしてしまう人を、何度もお見かけしました。よい筆はペインターにとって財産ですので、くれぐれも大切に取り扱って下さい。

●絵付け筆

私は絵を描くとき、一般的な平筆、丸筆のほか三田村商店の別製リス毛平筆を使っています。別製リス毛平筆は軟らかく適当な厚みがあるので、必要な絵の具をしっかり塗りながらスムーズなぼかし表現をすることができます。つまり、作品を少ない焼成回数で仕上げたい場合にも大変適しています。難点としては毛先の揃いがあまりよくないので、私は使用前にハサミでカットして揃えてから使っています。その際、カットし過ぎるとかえって使いにくい筆になってしまいますので、飛び出ている先端部分を少し切りそろえる程度にします。細かい線描には白毛判下筆（ディテールライナー）を使います。

日本で市販されている平筆は大変性能がよいと思うのですが、14号以上の大きい絵付け用平筆の種類が少ないのが残念です。大きいモチーフを美しく描くには必然的に大きな平筆が必要ですので、私は特大の平筆は海外の通販などから購入しています。

絵を描くときには筆は可能な限り大きなものを使うことをお勧めします。小さな筆で広い面積を何度もいじると筆跡が付き、埃も入りやすくなります。幅広の筆を使い最少の筆回しで仕上げることで、時間の節約ができるうえ、きれいな仕上がりが期待できます。

アメリカンチャイナペインティング特有のワイプアウト（抜き）の表現をする場合には化学繊維の平筆や丸筆も使います。

●ペンとペンオイル

繊細な模様を描いたりサインを入れるときなどは、絵付け材料店で販売されているペンを使います。

ペンオイルは絵付け材料店で入手できるものを使いますが、手元にないときや、ペインティングオイルで溶いてある絵の具を生かしたいときには、テレピンやクローブオイルなどを絵の具に少量足して即席のインクを作る場合があります。この方法は大変手軽で、わざわざペンオイルで絵の具を溶き直す必要がないので、お勧めです。

また、少量の粉砂糖と水で絵の具を溶き、ペンオイルの代わりにすることもあります。この砂糖水で溶く方法では、絵の具が早く乾くので接触による失敗を防ぐことができます。その際、粉砂糖と絵の具の割合は1：5程度です。

いずれの場合にも、ペン先の中にナイフでしっかりと溶いた絵の具をため込んでから使うと線が長持ちします。また、少し寝かせ気味にペンを使うとなめらかに描けます。ペンオイルは乾きやすいので作業中もペン先は筆洗いでまめに洗い、ペン先がつぶれてきたら躊躇せず取り換えることが大切です。

●金

私は普段は日本製の19％の液状のマット金を使用しています。手ごろな価格で使いやすいのが、その理由です。金で豪華さを演出したい場合には30％あるいは

have to adapt with new kinds of oils occasionally.

I separate the brushes for water-based medium, gold and luster, from the other brushes.

Brush care is very important as most of painting brushes are so delicately made from soft animal hair. For hobby painters who do not paint every day, there is a tendency to neglect the care of brushes, which leads easily to ruined brushes. When the brushes become too dry due to a long period of non-usage, brush hair comes out. Keep in mind that good brush condition is the foundation of good painting.

Painting brush

Mitamura's square shader made from squirrel is my best brush for 1-firing technique. As it is very soft and supple, I can apply enough paints to complete a single motif just with one-firing. The only imperfection is the unevenness of the hair brush. I trim it just little bit carefully by myself to make it even. Detail liner brush made from cat hair is one of my favorite brushes to make delicate line. I also use many regular brushes bought from general suppliers. For large areas I recommend you to use the largest brush for easy control. It is hard to make smooth surface with small brushes. Large brushes can cover wide areas on the porcelain and make the surface smooth with just few strokes. Then we can save the time and energy to produce nice results. Some synthetic brushes are also convenient for doing "wipe out."

Pen and pen oil

Regular pen bought from general supplier is enough good for pen work.

I can get nice regular pen oil also from general supplier, I sometimes make instant pen oil to mix small amount of turpentine or clove oil with painting oil. It is convenient way when you need just a little ink.

I also like making pen ink from sugar water to mix paint and powder sugar 5:1 with water. As this ink dry fast, it is convenient to continue complicated work without firing. If you put enough ink inside of the nib, the ink keeps long. To get smooth drawing, use the pen with slanting position, clean the nib sometimes and do not hesitate to change worn nib.

Gold

Japanese 19% liquid mat gold is my favorite as it has enough brilliance to use with modern technique and furthermore easy to use. When I like to express gorgeous texture, 30% and 45% mat gold are also in my choice. 11% bright gold is my companion to play with miscellaneous technique such as ceramic painting gold underlay or chipping off, etc.

As gold dry fast, occasionally I take out small amount and lay on the tile. When gold dries, I mix just a few drops of gold thinner into the gold mixture to remake the condition. Mat gold should be used on the tile as we

45％のマット金を使うこともあります。また、安価な11％のブライト金液（赤金）も場面に応じて積極的に使います。

　金は乾きが早いので、その都度必要な量を出して使います。乾いてきたら金油など希釈オイルを少量足します。マット金を出す際に小皿を使うと金油を足した後の「練り直し」の作業がうまくできないので、必ず専用のタイルを使います。新しい金は金油で薄める必要はありません。残った金は瓶に戻さずタイルごと密封容器に入れ、次に使う際に金油で柔らかくして練り直すと、無駄なく使い切ることができます。金油が多いと金が薄まり、きれいに発色しません。場合によっては紫色になるので、金油は常に必要最低量を足すことを心がけて下さい。作業中、筆の中でも金が固まってきますから、タイルの上の金を練り直すタイミングで筆も金油で洗い、滑らかに使える状態に戻しましょう。

◇19％マット金

　液状のマット金を使う際には、毎回ナイフや棒で瓶の中をよく撹拌し、沈んでいる金粉と金液を均等にしてから使うことが大切です。一般には、金油は金属を溶かす性質があるので、撹拌にはプラスチックのナイフやガラス棒を使う方がよいといわれていますが、私はステンレスのスプーンやナイフでかき混ぜて、問題を感じたことはありません。薄刃のステンレスの道具を使うと、隅にたまった金粉も平均的によく混ぜることができます。使用前にこの撹拌作業を怠ると、最初と最後で金の質感が大きく異なり本来の質感を表現できないことになります。

　濃度の目安は、塗った色がコーヒー色であれば適量です。19％のマット金をベタ塗りする場合には周囲をマスキングし、平筆で塗った後、乾かないうちにスポンジで軽くパディングします。そうすることで、焼成後に絹のような均等な光沢を得ることができます。

◇30％、45％マット金

　30％や45％のマット金は、黒に近い濃い茶色であらかじめペースト状に練られています。濃度が高く1回で必要量をしっかりと塗ることができるので、作業の手間も省けます。19％のマット金は1回の塗布ではむらが目立ち結局2回塗るような場合もありますから、考え方次第ではお得な金であるといえます。近年の金価格の高騰で大変高価になり、手が出にくくなってしまったのが残念です。

◇11％ブライト金（赤金）

　11％のブライト金はラスターの仲間であり、焼成前は紅茶色をしています。金粉は含まれていないので、撹拌の必要はありません。取り出す際にもタイルの上ではなく、小皿で均等に混ぜることができます。塗った際に多少のむらがあっても、大抵の場合焼成後には均等な輝きを得ることができます。失敗が少なく、初心者向きといえるでしょう。光り方が派手なのであまり好まれない方も多いのですが、金下マットの上に塗る場合や陶器に使う場合には落ち着いたほどよいマット感を得ることができ、用途多様な便利な金だと思います。

◇金粉

　モダンな作品をつくるときには金粉を使うこともあります。繊細でマットな線を描きたい場合には、金粉を揮発性の速乾性メディウムで溶いてペン描きします。パディングして蒔絵のような表現に使うこともあります。

◇水溶性の金

have to mix it with the knife every five minutes. Never dilute new liquid gold with the thinner, as it is already in the best condition from the bottle. Dilute liquid gold only if the liquid becomes sticky because of evaporation. Do not return the used remaining gold back into the original bottle rather gather it together on the tile then store into a sealed plastic case. You can use this one at the next gold work with the few drops of gold thinner. Due to much gold thinner, gold quality becomes dull moreover the gold color turns to violet. Be careful not to use too much gold thinner.

During gold work, gold becomes sticky also in the brush. Clean the brush with the thinner at the same frequency as the repeated gold mixing.

19% liquid mat gold

Before using 19% liquid mat gold, it is very important to stir with a knife or a stainless steel rod so that the precipitated gold residue at the bottom of the bottle is evenly mixed in the bottle. Generally, people say that it is better to use glass or plastic tools for mixing gold rather than metal tools as the metal dissolves in the gold thinner. However, I have no problem so far using stainless steel tools with gold, on the contrary I think metal tools are functional than plastic one to make the obstinate gold gentle.

The best color of un-fired 19% liquid mat gold is European coffee color. When I need a flat texture of this gold, resist outside the motif before painting, and paint gold on the space, padding gently with a sponge. Then a silky texture of the gold is obtained.

30% and 45% mat gold

30% or 45% mat gold comes already mixed as black paste. As the concentration of the gold is very high, we can paint enough gold almost with one stroke. We can save the time and energy with this gold, as sometimes we have to paint twice using 19% mat gold to get a satisfactory result.

11% liquid bright gold

11% liquid bright gold is a companion of luster as it looks like English tea color before firing and it is not necessary to stir before painting. All painters can get brilliant gold color easily with this gold. This gold is good for beginner. However, some people do not prefer this gold as they think it is too vulgar. Try painting this gold on gold underlay or ceramic, it looks placid with this poor gold. That's why I prefer this gold, since my mind is challenged to think of an effective way to use for my design.

Gold powder

Gold powder also brings me nice imagination in painting modern design. This powder is real gold powder which can be used with pen work or padding with a sponge like gold lacquer.

Water-based gold

We can get many kinds of water-based gold

最近では水溶性のマット金も様々なタイプのものが市販されており、油性のものに比べても、使用後の質感は遜色ありません。多少割高ですが、水溶性のオイルや水で希釈できるので、取り扱いが簡単で匂いもありません。アレルギー体質の方には特にお勧めです。

◇プラチナ

液状のブライトプラチナとマットプラチナが市販されています。ブライトプラチナはラスターの仲間ですが、マットプラチナは金の仲間です。それぞれブライト金、マット金に準じた方法で取り扱って下さい。ただし、プラチナは金以上に希釈による質感の衰えが目立つので、金油で希釈する際には少量ずつ慎重に行いましょう。

●金彩用の筆

繊細な金線を描く場合には、白毛判下筆（ディテールライナー）を使います。金盛り、スクロールなど様々な金細工用には各サイズ揃った「金用筆セット」も重宝します。広い面を塗る場合にはリス毛の平筆を使います。

●ラスター

ラスターはマット金液とは違い瓶の底に金属成分が沈殿することがないので、使用前に撹拌する必要はありません。ただし、特に日本製のラスターは最初からどろりとした状態で販売されているものが多いので、使うときには必要量を皿に取り、必ずラスター油で10～30％程度に薄めてサラサラの状態にしてから使用しましょう。ラスターがうまくいかない方は、大抵の場合ラスター油による希釈が足りないようです。薄過ぎるラスターは、塗り直し再焼成してきれいに修復することが可能ですが、厚塗りでボロボロにはがれたラスターを修復するのは困難です。

ヨーロッパ製のラスターなど最初からサラサラの状態のものは必ずしも薄める必要はありませんが、希釈をしない場合には大変強い色で発色する場合があります。希釈しながら色の調整をするとよいでしょう。加減は経験で覚えるしかありませんので、実験を重ねて最適な状態を会得して下さい。

ラスターは筆ではなくスポンジで直接塗ることもできますが、真珠ラスターはその特徴である虹色（イリデッセント）を出すために必ず筆で塗って下さい。丸筆を細かく動かして塗ることで、より華やかな色彩になります。

ラスターをより美しく仕上げるためには2度塗りすることをお勧めします。赤、紫、黒系のラスターは、わずか1年ほどで分離して使えない状態になることがあるので、できるだけ早く使い切って下さい。

●ラスター用の筆

化学繊維の筆、動物毛の筆、いずれの筆も使うことができます。広い面には平筆、真珠ラスターのイリデッセント用には丸筆を使います。

●金彩用筆とラスター用筆の手入れ

金彩用の筆やラスター用の筆は使用後金油やラスター油で汚れを落とし、絵付け筆同様に筆洗いで洗い、さらにアクアマジックで洗ってから水ですすぎ、陰干しします。このように丁寧に洗うことで、次に使う際、最良の状態ですぐに作業に取りかかることができます。

金彩用の筆を洗わずにラップに包んで保存し、次に使う際に金油で柔らかくして使用する方法もありますが、これは毎日のように金彩をするプロの方法です。た

from suppliers these years. Although the price is more expensive than that of regular gold, it is surely welcomed by people who have allergic problem. The fired result is as good as regular gold. As the thinner is water-based thinner or just water, it has no smell and it is easy to clean the tools.

Platinum
Japanese liquid bright platinum and liquid mat platinum are my choices of platinum source. Bright platinum is a companion of luster and mat platinum is a companion of gold. The use is almost the same as gold I described in the former paragraph. However, as the platinum is weaker for too much thinner than gold, be careful to thin especially.

Gold brushes
To draw delicate gold line, detail liner brush made from cat hair is the best. Gold brush set is also useful to do gold works and to paint over raised enamel or for scrolling. Square shader is also good for painting large areas.

Luster
We do not have to stir luster before using as they contain no metallic powder in it. As some of Japanese luster is sticky even it is fresh, we have to thin it with 10–30% luster thinner to make luster liquid smooth. I think some of failures in luster work, is caused by luster thinner as too much or too little. Too much thinner makes luster dull but we can repair it with a second coating getting a nice effect after second firing. Sticky coat destroy the luster surface as it comes off partially. Then it is too difficult to repair with the second firing.

Some of freshly opened European or American luster is in ideal liquid consistency, ready to use and it is not always necessary to thin. Moreover, the color intensity can be controlled with the thinner as one likes, whether a weak color or strong color. Luster can be applied directly with sponge, however be sure not to apply mother-of-pearl with sponge but with brush with a quivering motion to make iridescent rainbow-like effect.

I prefer double coating of luster which brings brilliant effect on the porcelain.

Although red, violet and black luster are spoiled in a short time, I do not keep luster in the refrigerator because I worry about toxic vapors coming from the bottle, I just rush to use them in a year. Experience is the best textbook for you about luster.

Luster brushes
Both synthetic and animal hair brushes can be used for luster work. I use a small round brush to apply mother-of-pearl luster in an iridescent brush technique. Square shader is also useful.

Care for gold brush and luster brush
I clean both brushes with thinner first, secondly clean with the regular brush cleaner, and thirdly I clean with Aqua Magic, finally I

まに金彩をするホビーペインターが同じようにすると、筆に付着した金を溶かそうと焦り、かえって筆を台無しにしてしまうことがあります。

金彩用の筆は絵付け用の筆と分けることが望ましいのですが、それが無理であれば、アクアマジックではなくアルコールで洗って完全に汚れを落として下さい。アルコールは短時間で揮発するので、すぐに別のオイルを筆に含ませることができます。ただし、アルコールには筆をケアする成分がないので、最終的な洗浄をアルコールに頼ると筆が乾燥して傷みます。

●焼成後の金やラスターのマスキング

複雑な細工を施す作品制作過程では、焼成後の金やラスターの上にマスキングする場合があります。

そのような場合に直接赤のマスキング液を塗ると、乾いた後、はがれなくなります。それを防ぐためには、マスキング液を塗る前にペーパータオルにテレピンを付けて金やラスターの上を軽く拭くとよいでしょう。そうすることでテレピンの薄い被膜がかかるので、作業後マスキングをはがしやすくなります。これはシールを使うマスキングでも同様で、シールを貼る前に白磁をテレピンで拭くと、作業後にシールをはがしやすくなります。

●金みがき

磨きの必要があるタイプのマット金は、焼成後に磨いて仕上げる必要があります。市販の磨き砂や金専用の紙やすりを使って光沢を出すこともできますが、ホームセンターで売っている工業用の金研磨用のクロス（＊注）は大変便利です。磨き砂と違って砂カスが出ない上、ソフトに隅々まできれいに磨くことができます。

＊注：株式会社光陽社の「研磨つや出し布ポリマール」

●焼成後の金の汚れを消したい場合

焼成前の掃除不足で紫色に焼き付いた金の汚れは専用の「金消し」で消すことができます。また、ヨードチンキを塗って拭き消すこともできます。

窯と焼成
Kiln and firing

●熱回り

設置環境が許されるならば、内部が円筒形に近く熱回りのよい窯を使うことをお勧めします。熱回りがスムーズでない場合、作品の置き場所によって焼きむらが生じます。つまり、同じ条件の作品でも上部に置いたものは艶がよいのに、下の方に置いたものは生焼けでマットな状態に仕上がるというようなことが起こります。熱回りのよい窯の中では、作品をどの場所においても艶のよい焼き上がりが期待できます。

●焼成温度

私はほとんどの場合780℃で焼成しています。300℃までは蓋を少し開けて換気しながら焼成します。最高温度での保持時間（ねらし）は0〜10分です。

---

rinse with water and dry naturally. Then I can always start painting any time with the best brush condition.

Some of the professional painters do not clean the gold brush. They just wrap it with cling film or keep it in the sealed case to protect from the dust, and at the next gold work, they soften the brush with gold thinner to use again. It is good for the professional painter to save the gold and also save the time as they paint gold almost everyday. However, not all hobby painters paint gold everyday. Often the brushes are ruined when they treat the brushes as professionals do with their brushes. When the brushes harden after their last gold work, it takes long time to soften the brushes. Most of hobby painters cannot be patient with such situation.

Apparently it is best to separate gold brushes from the painting brushes but in cases when you have to use the same brush for both purposes, clean the brush with alcohol. As alcohol is a strong cleaner and evaporates fast, you can use the same brush for another purpose temporary, but remember alcohol contains no essence to care for the brush hair.

Masking on the fired gold and fired luster

In the process of the complicated work, sometimes I have to resist the fired gold or fired luster. In this case, red resist is not directly applied on the gold or luster, because resist sticks strongly it may be difficult to take off the resist easily when it dries. Coat the gold or luster with a little bit of turpentine using tissue paper. The turpentine thin coating on the gold or luster helps in taking off the resist easily. This method is also effective for the stickers.

Sanding gold

High gold content mat gold should be sanded after firing. As you know sea sand and sand paper are convenient for polishing gold. The industrial cloth for polishing gold metal is also convenient as it is soft and brings no dust on the gold.

Erase the gold stain

Gold eraser and gold-off, a kind of toxic solution can erase fired gold completely. However, I recommend trying tincture of iodine as an eraser. Violet stain on the porcelain comes off easily with this solution.

Circulation

Air circulation in the kiln is essential for bringing a glossy finish to porcelains that is the reason why I love my round-shaped kiln because it has that efficiency. Without smooth air circulation, temperature is not even in the kiln resulting in differences in surface shine in the pieces set on the upper shelf from those pieces set on the lower shelf. After firing some pieces are mat and others are glossy.

780℃というのは私の窯では大変便利な温度で、この温度では高温を良とする金系の絵の具もきれいに発色し、低めの温度を良しとする鉄系の絵の具も焦げることがありません。しかも、同時に塗布したエナメルや金もひび割れを起こさずに、きれいな仕上がりが期待できる温度です。ただし、絵の具の上に金を塗るとき、レイズドペーストなど低温焼成が必要な盛りを使う場合は例外で、この温度からさらに10～20℃下げて焼成します。

　本書で述べている温度は全て一般的な磁器を焼成する場合の温度なので、ボーンチャイナなど軟質磁器に絵付けする場合には全て10～20℃低い設定で焼成を行って下さい。また、硬質磁器絵付けには20℃ぐらい高い温度で焼成すると、金系の色（マロン、バイオレット、ピンクなど）はより鮮やかに発色します。

　完成まで数回の焼成が必要と思われる作品では、最終焼成のみ10分の温度保持時間を設定し、それまでの焼成では温度保持時間は設定しません。ただし、焼成ごとに温度を下げる焼成を行う場合には、その都度10分の温度保持時間を設定します。

　ブラックやマロンなど金系の絵の具やメタリック絵の具を厚塗りした場合、焼成回数が増えるほど剥離のリスクが高まります。厚塗りが懸念される場合、これらの絵の具は多くても3回以内の焼成に抑えて下さい。剥離面の修正では、食器以外に用いたメタリック絵の具のみ720℃以下の低温焼成で修復することが可能です。

　770℃以下の低温焼成の場合、ブルー系、金系の絵の具は艶が出ずマットな仕上がりになるので、手順を考えてリスクの少ない焼成を行うように心がけて下さい。

● 焼成のトラブル

　窯の内部で磁器周りの空気の流れが悪いと、滞った空気との温度差が原因でまれに磁器が割れることがあります。皿や陶板を焼成する場合には、対流の死角を作らないように、耐熱鋼鉄製の三角棚を使うことをお勧めしますが、陶器の棚板に直接皿や陶板を乗せる場合には、トチを使って棚板との間に少しすきまを作ることで空気の流れを作り、割れにくくすることができます。また、形状が複雑な皿はその形自体が割れる原因になることがあります。磁器本体内の熱回りが偏り、内部で起こるアンバランスな膨張に耐えきれずに割れてしまうわけです。

　800℃もの高温にさらされる焼成には「事故」が付きものです。どんなに注意しても、機械のトラブルや磁器や絵の具の状態で不本意な焼成結果になってしまうことはあります。私自身、最終焼成で作品をだめにしてしまったことも1度や2度ではありません。トラブルに見舞われても、それをよい経験として次の作品に生かすよう心がけたいものです。

　窯によって様々な「くせ」があり、私の窯で最適な温度や時間が、全ての窯でも最適とは限りません。ご自分の窯で焼成を重ね、様々な「くせ」を見抜いて下さい。私自身は米国製の窯を使っていますが、日本製の窯でも性能のよいものがありますので、設置条件も含め、ご自身に合った窯をお探し下さい。

　なお、耐熱鋼鉄製の三角棚は、イングレーズ焼成では使うことができません。

Temperature

The pieces are fired usually at 780℃ (cone 016). Ventilation is kept on till 300℃ and the keeping time of the maximum temperature is 0–10 minutes. I think 780℃ is really a convenient temperature. Gold colors and iron colors are both fine in this temperature and furthermore, enamel and gold are also safe with this temperature. In firing gold painted on the raised paste or on the fired paint, I reduce 20 from the usual firing temperature.

　Painting on soft china such as bone china is the exception. In all firings of soft china, I reduce the temperature 10–20 from the instructed temperature. Painting on hard china such as some of European porcelain, gold colors becomes brilliant when fired at 20–40 higher temperature than that of my regular firing.

　When I have to fire several times to complete the work, keeping time is not at the maximum temperature on each firing, only in the last firing. I only maintain 10 minutes keeping time at the final firing.

　Cases when I reduce maximum temperature step by step at each firing, I maintain keeping time at 10 minutes in every firing.

　When gold colors and other colors such as black, maroon and metallic are painted too thick, they may chip-off during firings. Fire them three times at maximum, to prevent chipping off. Although metallic paints can be repaired when fired at 700–720℃, blue and gold colors are not glossy under 770℃. It is advisable to plan well the best process of firing.

Trouble with firing

Accidentally, breaking of porcelain happens in the kiln during firing, caused by circulation problem around the porcelains. It is not good to place porcelain plates directly on the bottom ceramic flat stand. The hot air inside tends to be accumulated around the bottom of the plate and the temperature is much higher at the bottom than upper portion of the plate. Due to the differences in temperatures some porcelain are broken inside the kiln.

　You can get many kinds of accessories to set in the kiln, use them to create good circulation. Some of porcelains having unnoticeable defects to start with such as uneven shape cannot stand several firings. Due to the uneven thermal expansion, some of them are broken in the kiln. Firing problems are inevitable caused not only by kiln master but also by the machine. Never be disappointed with such results, consider it as one of the good experiences for good training.

　As every kiln has its own character, my best way may differ from your best way. Observe and know your kiln well through experiences with firing.

掲載作品に使用した絵の具と特殊材料一覧

絵の具の表記は主に原宿陶画舎のメインカラーシリーズの名称を使用していますが、他のメーカーの絵の具も同様にお使いいただけます。
(I)印はイングレーズ絵の具、(IR)印はイリデッセント絵の具、(M)印はメタリック絵の具、(E)印は花島悦子オリジナル絵の具です。
オリジナル絵の具は花島悦子から直接お買い求めいただけます。

p.6 伊万里風牡丹皿
染付ブルー(I)、ヘブンリーブルー(I)、伊万里ブルーNo.2(I)、パープルピンク、ライラックNo.2、ローズピンク、ローズマロンNo.2、クロムグリーン、インペリアルグリーン、ピーコックブルー、ネイプルスイエロー、ブラック、レッドブラウン(E)、シルバースノウ(M)、真珠ラスター、若草ラスター、ピーチラスター、エナメルフリット、19％マット金

p.8 四季の舞扇
ブラック、ホワイト、クタニレッド(E)、マルベリー、ネイプルスイエロー、クロムグリーン、インペリアルグリーン、チョコレートブラウン、オリーブグリーンNo.1、グレー、パープルピンク、ローズマロンNo.1、レッドブラウン(E)、ピーコックブルー、ロイヤルバイオレット、ライラックNo2、オリエントブルー、オーカー、イエローブラウン、シフォンブルー(M)、藤色ラスター、真珠ラスター、金茶ラスター、水色ラスター、ブルーマザーオブパールラスター、ブラックラスター、エナメルフリット、ガラスビーズS、19％マット金

p.10 菊の丸窓
染付ブルー(I)、ヘブンリーブルー(I)、伊万里ブルーNo.2(I)、パープルピンク、ローズピンク、マルベリー、ライラックNo.2、ロイヤルバイオレット、グレー、ネイプルスイエロー、イエローブラウン、オーカー、オリーブグリーンNo.1、クロムグリーン、アクセントグリーン、ピーコックブルー、シルバースノウ(M)、真珠ラスター、水色ラスター、エナメルフリット、19％マット金、マーブルローション

p.12 花園の鶴
ブラック、ホワイト、ロイヤルバイオレット、ピーコックブルー、グレー、クタニレッド(E)、パープルピンク、ライラックNo2、ローズマロンNo.1、ネイプルスイエロー、イエローブラウン、オーカー、クロムグリーン、アイアンレッド、メタリックゴールド(M)、メタリックシルバー(M)、ルビーブロンズ(M)、エナメルフリット、19％マット金

p.14 紅椿
アイアンレッド、ネイプルスイエロー、グリーンシャドウ(E)、ブラック、ホワイト、染付ブルー(I)、ヘブンリーブルー(I)、伊万里ブルーNo.2(I)、クタニレッド(E)、シルバースノウ(M)、オーロラスター、真珠ラスター、水色ラスター、エナメルフリット、19％マット金

p.16 青のハーモニー
染付ブルー(I)、ヘブンリーブルー(I)、伊万里ブルーNo2(I)、アイアンレッド、ブラック、19％マット金、マットプラチナ

p.17 沖の鶴
P.78参照

List of painting colors and materials

The paints are of the Main Color Series available from Harajuku Togasha.
The paints for over-glaze painting from the other suppliers can be used.
I: In-glaze paint; IR: Iridescent paints; M: Metallic paint; L: Luster; E: Etsuko's original paint
Etsuko supply her original paints and materials.

Naples Yellow = Mixing Yellow, Imperial Green = Darkest Green, metallic cold = fake gold, enamel frit = transparent enamel powder

p.6 Grand Imari
Sometsuke Blue(I), Heavenly Blue(I), Imari Blue No.2(I), Purple Pink, Lilac No.2, Rose Pink, Rose Maroon No.2, Chrome Green, Imperial Green, Peacock Blue, Naples Yellow, Black, Red Brown(E), Silver Snow(M), mother-of-pearl(L), green(L), peach(L), enamel frit, 19% mat gold

p.8 Four Seasons
Black, White, Kutani Red(E), Mulberry, Naples Yellow, Chrome Green, Imperial Green, Chocolate Brown, Olive Green No.1, Gray, Purple Pink, Rose Maroon No.1, Red Brown (E), Peacock Blue, Royal Violet, Lilac No.2, Orient Blue, Ocher, Yellow Brown, Chiffon Blue (M), Lilac (L), mother-of-pearl(L), gold brown (L), blue (L), blue mother-of-pearl (L), black (L), enamel frit, glass beads S, 19% mat gold

p.10 Round Windows of Chrysanthemums
Sometsuke Blue(I), Heavenly Blue (I), Imari Blue No.2 (I), Purple Pink, Rose Pink, Mulberry, Lilac No.2, Royal Violet, Gray, Naples Yellow, Yellow Brawn, Ocher, Olive Green No.1, Chrome Green, Accent Green, Peacock Blue, Silver Snow (M), mother-of-pearl (L), blue (L), enamel frit, 19% mat gold, marble lotion

p.12 Celestial Cranes
Black, White, Royal Violet, Peacock Blue, Gray, Kutani Red(E), Purple Pink, Lilac No.2, Rose Maroon No1, Naples Yellow, Yellow Brawn, Ocher, Chrome Green, Iron Red, metallic gold (M), metallic silver (M), ruby bronze (M), enamel frit, 19% mat gold

p.14 Red Camellia
Iron Red, Naples Yellow, Green Shadow (E), Black, White, Sometsuke Blue (I), Heavenly Blue (I), Imari Blue No.2 (I), Kutani Red (E), Silver Snow (M), aurora (L), mother-of-pearl (L), blue (L), enamel frit, 19% mat gold

p.16 Peonies in Blue Harmony
Sometsuke Blue (I), Heavenly Blue (I), Imari Blue No.2 (I), Iron Red, Black, 19% mat gold, mat platinum

p.17 A Crane on the Sea
Refer to P.78.

p.18 深海に牡丹
グレー、ライラックNo.2、パープルピンク、ローズピンク、マルベリー、ネイプルスイエロー、ダークグリーン、オリーブグリーンNo.1、インペリアルグリーン、ブラック、ホワイト、チョコレートブラウン、レッドブラウン（E）、グリーン、ロイヤルバイオレット、染付ブルー（I）、水色ラスター、エナメルフリット、19％マット金、マットプラチナ

p.19 宇宙のクリスマス
p. 72参照

p. 20, p. 21 暁の蓮・輝きの時
p. 75参照（2点とも同じ）

p. 22 夕暮れの藤
ライラックNo.2、パープルピンク、ロイヤルバイオレット、ネイプルスイエロー、アクアグリーン、ダークグリーン、ピーコックブルー、オリーブグリーンNo.1、インペリアルグリーン、レッドブラウン（E）、エナメルフリット、真珠ラスター、19％マット金、マットプラチナ、ガラスビーズL,M

p. 24 花の集い
ライラックNo.2、ロイヤルバイオレット、ピーコックブルー、パープルピンク、ローズピンク、ローズマロンNo.1、レモンイエロー、ネイプルスイエロー、グレー、イエローラスター、水色ラスター、マーブルローション、マット粉、エナメルフリット、19％マット金、ガラスビーズS

p. 25 椿のティーセット
クタニレッド（E）、ネイプルスイエロー、オリーブグリーンNo.1、インペリアルグリーン、メタリックゴールド（M）、シルバースノウ（M）、水色ラスター、エナメルフリット、19％マット金、ステンシル用シール

p. 26 紫陽花の花束
ピーコックブルー、ライラックNo.2、ロイヤルバイオレット、パープルピンク、ローズマロンNo.1、グレー、ネイプルスイエロー、ブラック、ホワイト、レッドブラウン（E）、エナメルフリット、真珠ラスター、19％マット金、ガラスチップ（イエロー）、ガラスビーズL,M

p. 28 籠の蝶々
ネイプルスイエロー、クロムグリーン、ピーコックブルー、ロイヤルバイオレット、パープルピンク、ローズピンク、ローズマロンNo.1、グレー、ブラック、ブラックラスター、エナメルフリット、マーブルローション、アイリーフ、19％マット金、ガラスビーズL,M,S

p. 29 蝶の宝石
ピーコックブルー、ロイヤルバイオレット、ローズマロンNo.1、ダークグリーン、ネイプルスイエロー、グレー、ブラック、メタリックゴールド（M）、エナメルフリット、マットプラチナ、ガラスビーズM

p.30 牡丹狂乱
マルベリー、ライラックNo.2、パープルピンク、ブルー、グレー、ネイプルスイエロー、オリーブグリーンNo.1、インペリアルグリーン、ホワイト、ブラック、マットブラック、ブラックラスター、エナメルフリット、19％マット金、ガラスチップ（グリーン）、ガラスビーズM

p. 32 朝露とクレマチス
ピーコックブルー、ネイプルスイエロー、ロイヤルバイオレット、オリーブグリーンNo.1、インペリアルグリーン、ブラック、真珠ラスター、水色ラスター、ブルーマザーオブパールラスター、エナメルフリット、19％マット金、ガラスビーズ丸粒、墨汁

p. 18 Peonies in the Deep Ocean
Gray, Lilac No.2, Purple Pink, Rose Pink, Mulberry, Naples Yellow, Dark Green, Olive Green No.1, Imperial Green, Black, White, Chocolate Brown, Red Brown (E), Green, Royal Violet, Sometsuke Blue (I), blue (L), enamel frit, 19% mat gold, mat platinum

p. 19 Cosmic Christmas
Refer to P.72.

p. 20, P.21 Heavenly Lotus, Golden Moment
Refer to p.75 for both pieces.

p. 22 Evening Wisteria
Lilac No.2, Purple Pink, Royal Violet, Naples Yellow, Aqua Green, Dark Green, Peacock Blue, Olive Green No.1, Imperial Green, Red Brawn (E), enamel frit, mother-of-pearl (L), 19% mat gold, mat platinum, glass beads L, M

p. 24 Floral Harmony in a Box
Lilac No.2, Royal Violet, Peacock Blue, Purple Pink, Rose Pink, Rose Maroon No1, Lemon Yellow, Naples Yellow, Gray, yellow (L), Blue (E), marble lotion, mat powder, enamel frit, 19% mat gold, glass beads S

p. 25 Camellias on Tea Set
Kutani Red (E), Naples Yellow, Olive Green No.1, Imperial Green, Metallic Gold (M), Silver Snow (M), blue (L), enamel frit, 19% mat gold, sticker for stencil

p. 26 Hydrangea Bouquet
Peacock Blue, Lilac No.2, Royal Violet, Purple Pink, Rose Maroon No.1, Gray, Naples Yellow, Black, White, Red Brawn (E), enamel frit, mother-of-pearl (L), 19% mat gold, glass tips (yellow), glass beads L, M

p. 28 Butterflies in a Basket
Naples Yellow, Chrome Green, Peacock Blue, Royal Violet, Purple Pink, Rose Pink, Rose Maroon No.1, Gray, Black, black (L), enamel frit, marble lotion, I-Relief, 19% mat gold, glass beads L, M, S

p. 29 Jeweled Butterfly
Peacock Blue, Royal Violet, Rose Maroon No.1, Dark Green, Naples Yellow, Gray, Black, metallic gold (M), enamel frit, mat platinum, glass beads M

p. 30 Strange-looking Peonies
Mulberry, Lilac No.2, Purple Pink, Blue, Gray, Naples Yellow, Olive Green No.1, Imperial Green, White, Black, Mat Black, black (L), enamel frit, 19% mat gold, glass tips (Green), glass beads M

p. 28 Clematis with Dewdrops
Peacock Blue, Naples Yellow, Royal Violet, Olive Green No.1, Imperial Green, Black, mother-of-pearl (L), blue (L), blue mother-of-pearl (L), enamel frit, 19% mat gold, round-shaped glass beads, Indian ink

p. 33 舞扇
マルベリー、ライラックNo.2、グレー、クロムグリーン、インペリアルグリーン、ネイプルスイエロー、ローズマロンNo.1、ブラック、ホワイト、ロイヤルバイオレット、メタリックシルバー(M)、メタリックゴールド(M)、エナメルフリット、19%マット金、マットプラチナ

p. 34 牡丹のコサージュ
パープルピンク、ローズピンク、ローズマロンNo.2、ライラックNo.2、ロイヤルバイオレット、ネイプルスイエロー、ホワイト、ブラック、レッドブラウン(E)、シルバースノウ(M)、真珠ラスター、エナメルフリット、19%マット金、マットプラチナ

p. 35 更紗牡丹
無色ラスター、シルバースノウ(M)、メタリックグリーン(M)、マーメイドグリーン(M)、マーメイドピンク(M)、ルミナスピンク(M)、ルビーブロンズ(M)、シフォンライラック(M)、メタリックゴールド(M)、メタリックシルバー(M)、ネイプルスイエロー、ロイヤルバイオレット、アイアンレッド、エナメルフリット、ガラスチップ(ブルー、グリーン)、ガラスビーズ丸3mm、ガラスビーズM

p. 36 睡蓮と鯉
グレー、アイアンレッド、ブラック、ネイプルスイエロー、ロイヤルバイオレット、ピーコックブルー、ネイプルスイエロー、オリーブグリーンNo.1、インペリアルグリーン、ブラックグリーンNo.2、レッドブラウン(E)、パープルピンク、ホワイト、イエローブラウン、オーカー、メタリックゴールド(M)、シルバースノウ(M)、真珠ラスター、ブルーマザーオブパールラスター、エナメルフリット

p. 42 蓮の小皿
パープルピンク、ローズピンク、オリーブグリーンNo.1、インペリアルグリーン、ネイプルスイエロー、エナメルフリット、19%マット金、ガラスビーズM

p. 48 墨はじきを応用したミニ・クリスマスプレート
赤色ラスター、墨汁

p. 52 椿のボックス
メタリックゴールド、ブラック、ローズマロンNo.2、ウォームピンク、クロムグリーン、インペリアルグリーン、ホワイト、エナメルフリット

p. 53 蒔絵風のボックス
ブラック、メタリックゴールド(M)、エナメルフリット

p. 54 イリデッセントの椿
ブラック、サファイア(IR)、アメジスト(IR)、メタリックゴールド(M)、ホワイト、エナメルフリット

p. 55 イリデッセントの紫陽花
ローズピンク、ロイヤルバイオレット、ピーコックブルー、クロムグリーン、インペリアルグリーン、アップルグリーン、ルビー(IR)、サファイア(IR)、アメジスト(IR)、ペリドット(IR)、メタリックゴールド(M)、ブラック、ホワイト、エナメルフリット

p. 29 Fans for Japanese Dance
Mulberry, Lilac No. 2, Gray, Chrome Green, Imperial Green, Naples Yellow, Rose Maroon No.1, Black, White, Royal Violet, metallic silver (M), metallic gold (M), enamel frit, 19% mat gold, mat platinum

p. 34 Peony Corsage
Purple Pink, Rose Pink, Rose Maroon No. 2, Lilac No. 2, Royal Violet, Naples Yellow, White, Black, Red Brown (E), Silver Snow (M), mother-of-pearl (L), enamel frit, 19% mat gold, mat platinum

p. 35 Chiffon Peonies
white (L), Silver Snow (M), Metallic Green (M), Mermaid Green (M), Mermaid Pink (M), Luminous Pink (M), Ruby Bronze (M), Chiffon Lilac (M), metallic gold (M), metallic silver (M), Naples Yellow, Royal Violet, Iron Red, enamel frit, glass tips (blue, green), round-shaped glass beads, glass beads M

p. 36 Carp with Water Lilies
Gray, Iron Red, Black, Naples Yellow, Royal Violet, Peacock Blue, Naples Yellow, Olive Green No.1, Imperial Green, Black Green No. 2, Red Brown (E), Purple Pink, White, Yellow Brown, Ocher, metallic gold (M), Silver Snow (M), mother-of-pearl (L), blue mother-of-pearl (L), enamel frit

p. 42 Lotus
Purple Pink, Rose Pink, Olive Green No.1, Imperial Green, Naples Yellow, enamel frit, 19% mat gold, glass beads M

p. 48 A small Christmas plate painted with Indian ink
Red (L), Indian ink

p. 52 Gold and Camellia
Metallic Gold (M), Black, Rose Maroon No. 2, Warm Pink, Chrome Green, Imperial Green, White, enamel frit

p. 53 Raised Metallic Gold on Black Box
Black, metallic gold (M), enamel frit

p. 54 Iridescent Camellia
Black, Sapphire(IR), Amethyst(IR), metallic gold(M), White, enamel frit

p. 55 Iridescent Hydrangea
Rose Pink, Royal Violet, Peacock Blue, Chrome Green, Imperial Green, Apple Green, Ruby (IR), Sapphire (IR), Amethyst (IR), Peridot (IR), metallic gold (M), Black, White, enamel frit

下絵集

本文に掲載した作品の一部の下絵です。
掲載頁と縮小率を示しています。

Sketch Collection

These are reduced size sketches of the works in this book.
The page number is shown and also the reduced size.

p. 6　伊万里風牡丹皿
Grand Imari
(70%)

p. 8 四季の舞扇
Four Seasons
(70%)

p.16 青のハーモニー
Peonies in Blue Harmony
(60%)

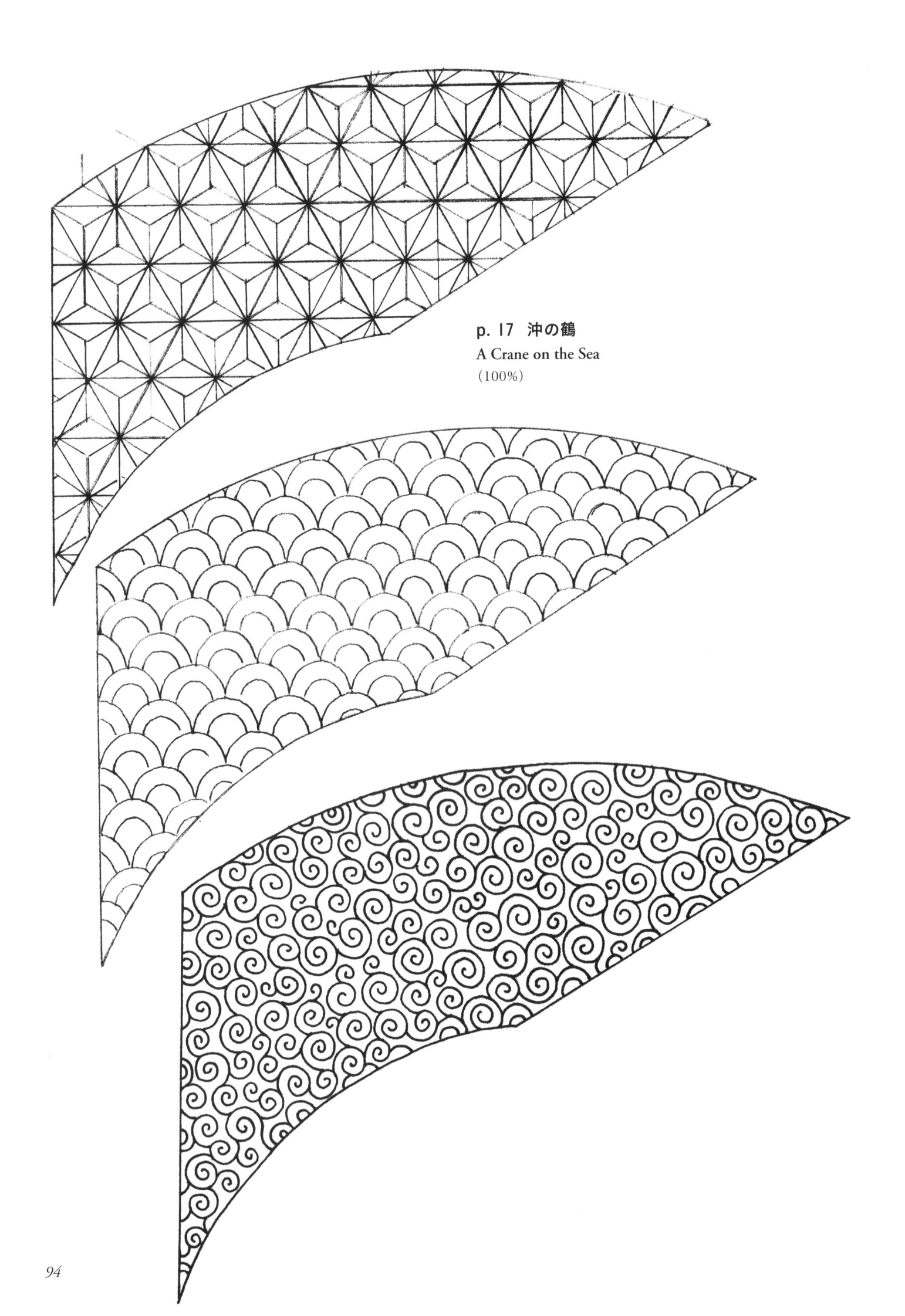

p. 17 沖の鶴
A Crane on the Sea
（100%）

95

p. 17 沖の鶴
A Crane on the Sea
(90%)

p. 19 宇宙のクリスマス
Cosmic Christmas
(70%)

97

p. 20 暁の蓮
Heavenly Lotus
(70%)

p. 24 花の集い
Floral Harmony in a Box
(100%)

p. 25 椿のティーセット
Camellias on Tea Set
(100%)

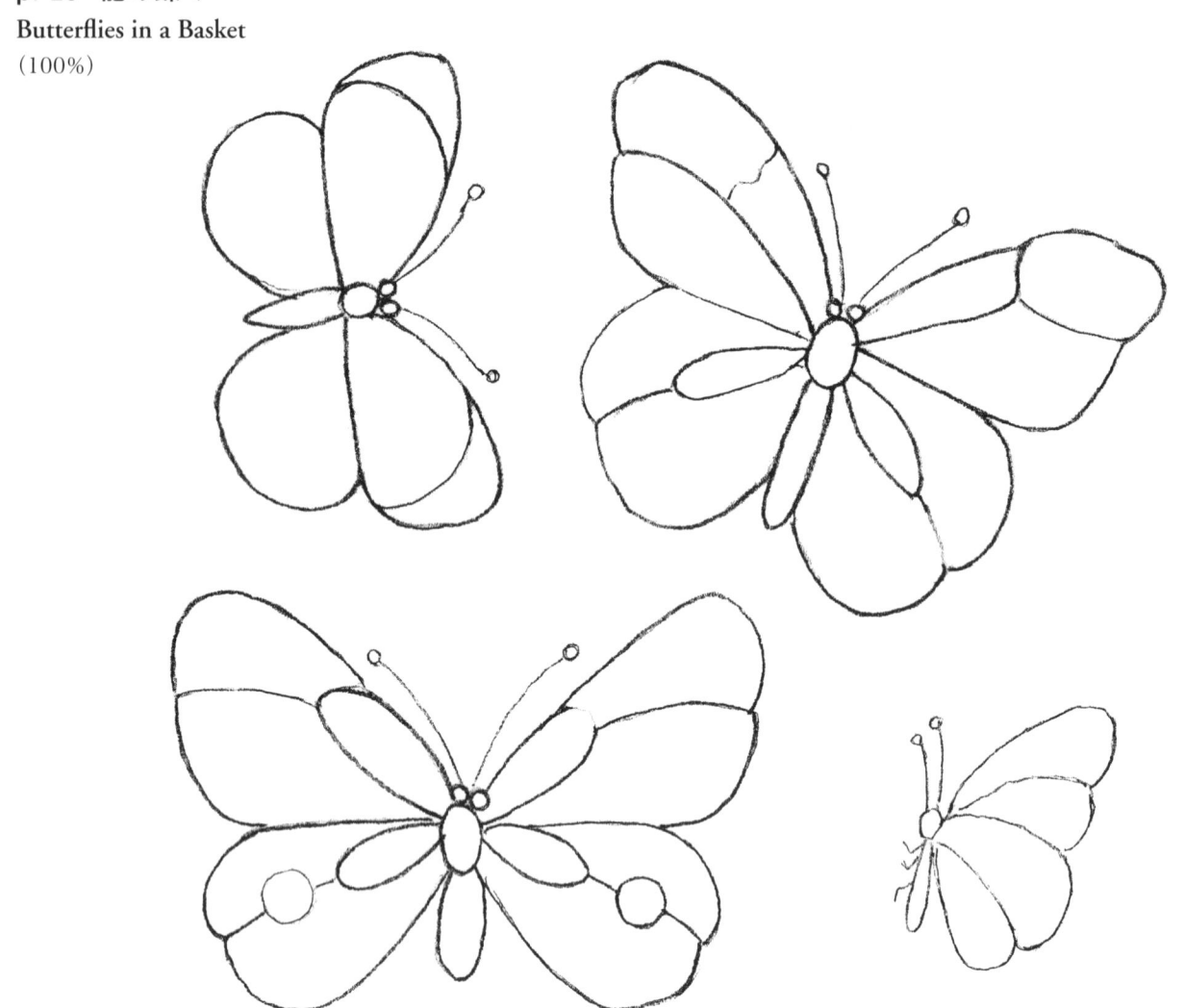

p. 28 籠の蝶々
Butterflies in a Basket
（100%）

p. 29 蝶の宝石
Jeweled Butterfly
（100%）

p. 30 牡丹狂乱
Strange-looking Peonies
（90%）

p. 32 朝露とクレマチス
Clematis with Dewdrops
(100%)

p. 33 舞扇

Fans for Japanese Dance

(90%)

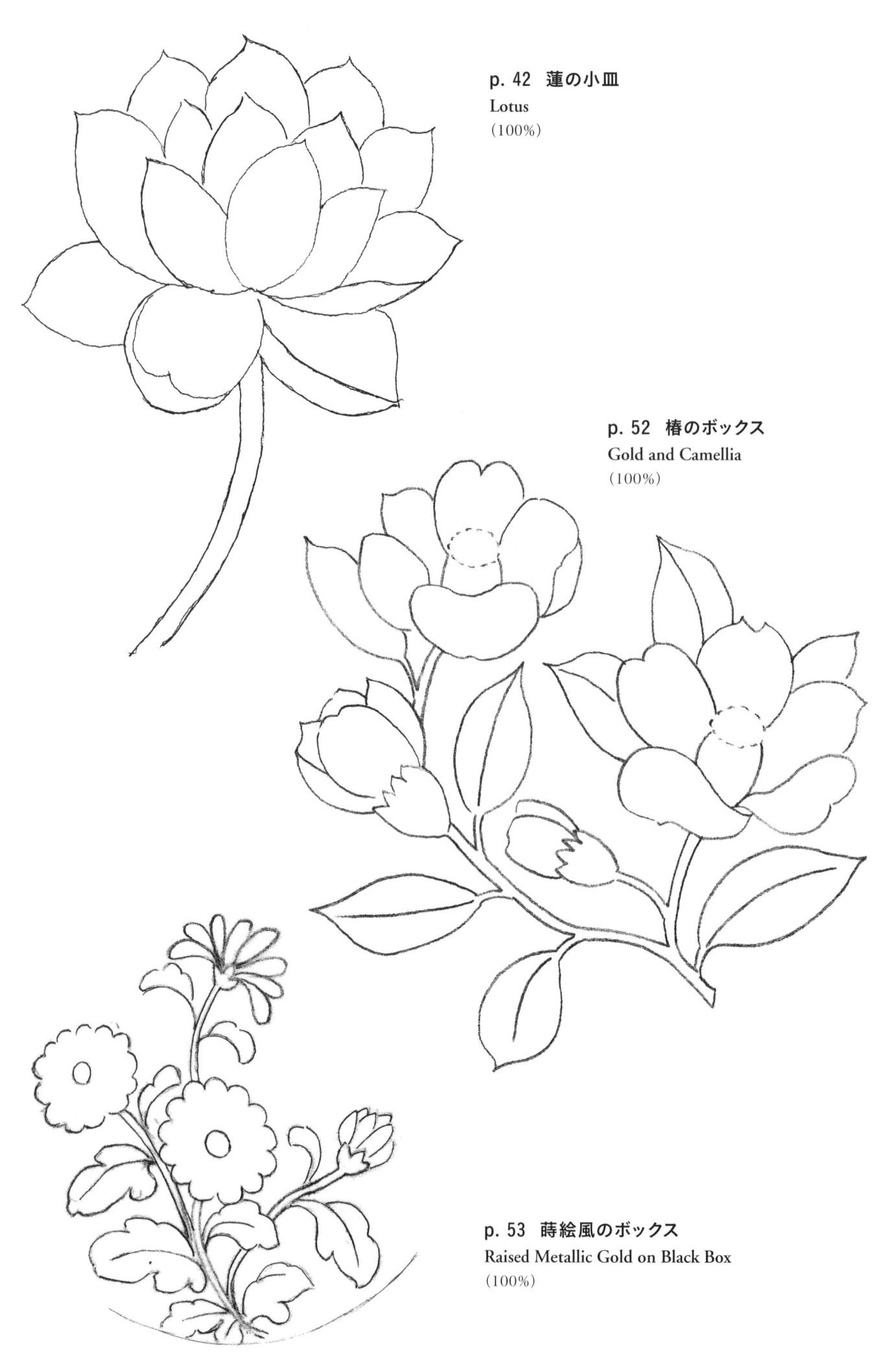

p. 42 蓮の小皿
Lotus
（100%）

p. 52 椿のボックス
Gold and Camellia
（100%）

p. 53 蒔絵風のボックス
Raised Metallic Gold on Black Box
（100%）

p. 56 マーガレット
Marguerite
(90%)

p. 56 ワイルドローズ
Wild Rose
(90%)

p. 56 芍薬
Peony
(90%)

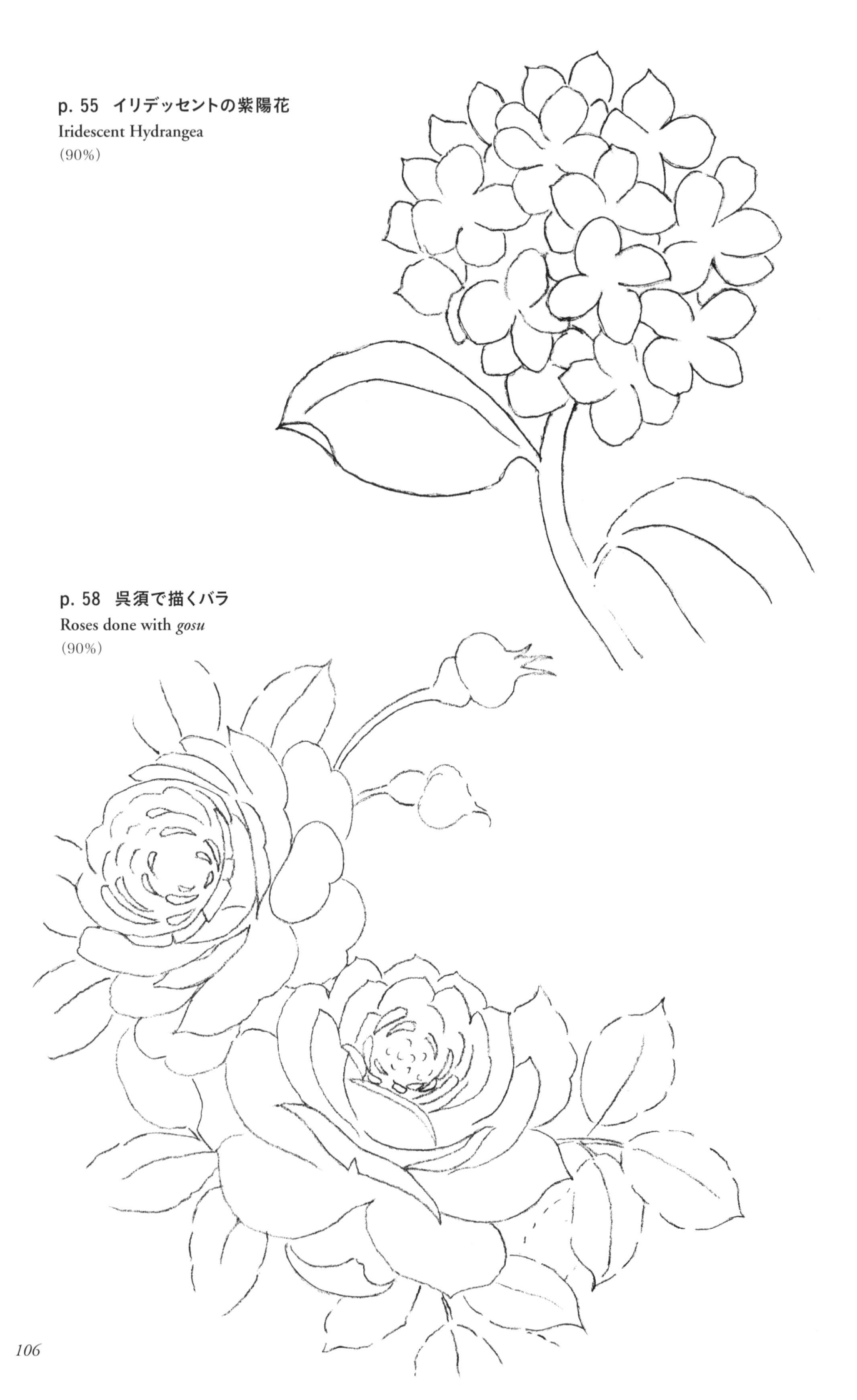

p. 55 イリデッセントの紫陽花
Iridescent Hydrangea
（90%）

p. 58 呉須で描くバラ
Roses done with *gosu*
（90%）

p. 60　鯉と蓮の葉の皿
Carp and lotus leaves
(70%)

107

p. 64　霜降り模様の鶴の皿
A Crane with Frosty Texture
（100%）

p. 68　牡丹の丸皿
A Peony with Black Rope
(70%)

絵付けの用具・材料取扱店 (50音順)　Tools and materials shop list

■**KILN ART SHOP & STUDIO サンアート (日本ヴォーグ社)**
〒162-8705　東京都新宿区市谷本村町 3-23　ヴォーグビル5F
TEL. (03) 5261-8265　FAX. (03) 5261-3638
http://sunart.exblog.jp/
KILN ART SHOP & STUDIO SUNART (NIHON VOGUE-SHA Co., Ltd.)
5F 3-23 Ichigayahommura-Cho, Shinjuku-Ku, Tokyo
162-8705 Japan

■**陶絵付学院 原宿陶画舎**
〒150-0001　東京都渋谷区神宮前 1-11-11
原宿グリーンファンタジアビル
TEL. (03) 3796-3013　FAX. (03) 3796-7800
http://www.togasha.com/
Harajuku TOGASHA
1-11-11 Jingu-mae, Shibuya-Ku, Tokyo 150-0001 Japan

■**株式会社三田村商店**
〒461-0012　愛知県名古屋市東区相生町 85
TEL. (052) 931-5564　FAX. (052) 932-1798
http://www.mitamura.co.jp
MITAMURA SHOTEN Co., Ltd.
85 Aioi-Cho, Higashi-Ku, Nagoya-City, Aichi
461-0012 Japan

■**ユザワヤ (蒲田店)**
〒144-8660　東京都大田区西蒲田 8-23-5
TEL. (03) 3734-4141　FAX. (03) 3730-8686
http://www.yuzawaya.co.jp
Yuzawaya Shoji Co., Ltd.
8-23-5 Nishi-kamata, Ohta-Ku, Tokyo
144-8660 Japan

おわりに

　前著『ポーセリン・アートの装飾テクニック』を書き終えた時には、自分の中の絵付けに関する全てを出しきって、もう自分は空っぽになってしまったというような感覚を覚えたものでした。しかし時がたち、再び時計の針が動き出すと、まるで枯井戸に水が満ちるように、どこからともなく別のアイディアが浮かんできて私の筆は再び止まらなくなりました。出版をきっかけに、思いがけなく国内、国外各方面からのお誘いが増え、世界中の人たちと絵付けの情熱を分かち合う機会にも恵まれました。そのような機会を通じて私の中の無限の未知なるスイッチが様々に反応したのであろうと思います。

　振り返り、私は特別に絵付けを学ぶために恵まれた人間であることを深く自覚しています。私にラスターの基礎を教えてくださった林緑先生、モダンテクニックの世界へと導いて下さったマーレイン・ジャコパン先生など、いつも丁度良いタイミングで良い方々との出会いがあり今に至りました。そうした積み重ねをもとに編み出した技法は、可能な限り世に広めていきたい。それが原点にある思いです。

　再び出版に至る長丁場にお付き合いくださった株式会社日貿出版社の川崎和美さん、英文チェックを引き受けてくださったグロリェッタ・イシザキ氏に深く感謝申し上げます。

2014年7月

花島 悦子

Gratitude

After the publication of my first book, I felt an emptiness. However, after a few months, once again new ideas came into my mind as if water was filling an empty well. I had the urge to paint again and I got busy.

　Through my former book, I was able to share my passion for porcelain painting with the international community of painters all over the world and as a result there was a demand for my techniques and am often invited internationally to teach. Those experiences continue to give me energy to produce new ideas.

　I believe I was born to learn and teach porcelain painting. God gave me several chances to meet the right people at the right timing. Especially I thank Mrs. Midori Hayashi who taught me the basic of the luster and Mrs. Marlene Jacopin who led me to the world of the modern techniques.

　As my techniques are the fruits of those experiences, I feel the responsibility to share those fruits to all painters in the world. That's why I publish.

　Special thanks to Ms. Kazumi Kawasaki of Japan Publications, Inc. and Ms. Glorietta Ishizaki to support me again to complete this great mission.

July 2014

Etsuko Hanajima

著者略歴

明治大学文学部卒業。
商社勤務を経て、1990年代半ば頃より絵付けの道へ入る。
2011年、株式会社日貿出版社より『ポーセリン・アートの装飾テクニック』出版。
2014年、米国に本拠を置く世界最大の絵付けスクール〈GA Seminars by the Sea〉より初の日本人講師として招待される。
フローラポーセリンスタジオ(自宅教室・軽井沢教室)主宰。
http://www.floraporcelainstudio.jp/

■ 資格

厚生労働省認定一級陶磁器技能士（絵付け作業）
IPATマスターアーティスト・マスターティーチャー
原宿陶画舎西洋絵付講師資格

■ 受賞歴

2002年　陶画舎展審査員特別賞
2002年　IPATロサンジェルス大会銀賞
2006年　IPATフィラデルフィア大会銀賞
2008年　IPATナッシュビル大会金賞
2010年　陶画舎展芸術優秀賞
2010年　IPATダラス大会金賞
2012年　陶画舎展陶画舎大賞
2012年　IPATサンフランシスコ大会金賞

■ 講師歴

原宿陶画舎分室講師、セミナー講師
株式会社日本ヴォーグ社セミナー講師
GA Seminars by the Sea（米国絵付けスクール）招待講師
その他、国内及び香港、シンガポール、オーストラリア、米国での招待講師歴多数

■ 所属団体

JPACジェイパック (Japan Porcelain Artists' Club) ボード会員
日本ポーセリンペインターズ協会 (JPPA) 会員
International Porcelain Artist & Teachers Inc. (IPAT) 会員

Profile

Etsuko Hanajima was born and raised in Japan.
　Although she experienced several art forms since her teenage years, porcelain painting fascinated her strongly, which led her to be professional artist.
　She published her first book *The Eclectic Sense of East-West Porcelain Art Decoration* (*Porcelain Art no Soshoku Techniques*) from Japan Publications, Inc. in 2011.
　She is the first Japanese teacher invited at GA Seminars by the Sea in 2014.
　Etsuko is now teaching at her studios in Tokyo and Karuizawa periodically and accept seminar requests internationally.

http://www.floraporcelainstudio.jp/

Certification:
First Class Level of the National Qualification of Painting Experts in Japan
IPAT Master Artist and Master Teacher
Certified Teacher of Harajuku Togasha

Awards:
2002 Togasha Exhibition in Tokyo, Japan: Special Prize from the Judge
2002 IPAT Convention in Los Angeles, USA: Silver Prize
2006 IPAT Convention in Philadelphia, USA: Silver Prize
2008 IPAT Convention in Nashville, USA: Gold Prize
2010 Togasha Exhibition in Tokyo, Japan: Excellent Art Prize
2010 IPAT Convention in Dallas, USA: Gold Prize
2012 Togasha Exhibition in Tokyo, Japan: Togasha Grand Prize
2012 IPAT Convention in San Francisco, USA: Gold Prize

Etsuko's seminar locations:
Harajuku Togasha in Tokyo, Japan
(C)Nihon Vogue-Sha Co., Ltd in Tokyo, Japan
GA Seminars by the Sea in Georgia, USA
Hong Kong, Singapore, Australia, USA (Michigan, California, Illinois), etc.

Membership:
Japan Porcelain Artists' Club (JPAC)
Japan Porcelain Painter's Association (JPPA)
International Porcelain Artists & Teachers, Inc. (IPAT)

本書の内容の一部あるいは全部を無断で複写複製（コピー）することは法律で認められた場合を除き、著作者および出版社の権利の侵害となりますので、その場合は予め小社あて許諾を求めて下さい。

ポーセリンアートの和モダンテクニック
作品づくりのための装飾アイディア　●定価はカバーに表示してあります

2014年8月8日　初版発行

著　者　　花島悦子
発行者　　川内長成
発行所　　株式会社日貿出版社

東京都文京区本郷 5-2-2　〒113-0033
電話（03）5805-3303（代表）
FAX（03）5805-3307
振替　00180-3-18495

印刷　　株式会社ワコープラネット
撮影　　松岡伸一
英文校正　グロリエッタ・イシザキ
装丁・本文レイアウト　株式会社オメガコム
©2014 by Etsuko Hanajima ／ Printed in Japan
落丁・乱丁本はお取替えいたします。

ISBN978-4-8170-8198-8　http://www.nichibou.co.jp/